LUKE

LUKE:
JESUS AND THE OUTSIDERS, OUTCASTS, AND OUTLAWS

978-1-7910-3131-2
978-1-5018-0804-3 *eBook*
978-1-5018-0805-0 *Large Print*

DVD
978-1-5018-0811-1

Leader Guide
978-1-5018-0806-7
978-1-5018-0807-4 *eBook*

Download a free children's leader guide, youth study, and reading plan at AdamHamilton.com/Luke

Also by Adam Hamilton

24 Hours That Changed the World

Christianity and World Religions

Christianity's Family Tree

Confronting the Controversies

Creed

Enough

Faithful

Final Words from the Cross

Forgiveness

Half Truths

Incarnation

John

Leading Beyond the Walls

Living Unafraid

Love to Stay

Making Sense of the Bible

Moses

Not a Silent Night

Prepare the Way for the Lord

Revival

Seeing Gray in a World of Black and White

Simon Peter

Speaking Well

The Call

The Journey

The Lord's Prayer

The Walk

The Way

Unafraid

When Christians Get It Wrong

Words of Life

Why?

For more information, visit AdamHamilton.com.

ADAM HAMILTON

Author of *John*, *The Walk*, and *24 Hours That Changed the World*

LUKE

JESUS AND THE OUTSIDERS, OUTCASTS, AND OUTLAWS

Abingdon Press | Nashville

To the people of Faith Chapel Assembly of God,
who welcomed and loved me when I was
a fourteen-year-old outsider
and who encouraged me to read
and study the Bible,
including the Gospel of Luke.
I will be forever grateful.

CONTENTS

INTRODUCTION

JESUS'S FRIENDS IN LOW PLACES

Many people have already applied themselves to the task of compiling an account of the events that have been fulfilled among us. They used what the original eyewitnesses and servants of the word handed down to us. Now, after having investigated everything carefully from the beginning, I have also decided to write a carefully ordered account for you, most honorable Theophilus. I want you to have confidence in the soundness of the instruction you have received.

(Luke 1:1-4)

I turned fourteen in the summer of 1978 and was preparing to begin high school that fall. My parents had divorced a couple of years earlier. My mom remarried a guy who was kind and who I really loved…when he wasn't drinking. We'd experienced drunken rages where my stepdad took a sledgehammer to the inside of our house as we were told to be quiet and eat our supper. I'd come home from school with my stepdad's stuff on the front lawn. We moved to three homes in two years. I knew no one I would be attending high school with. I felt alone, lonely, and sad. And if you would have asked about my faith that summer, I would have told you with great conviction that I was an atheist.

Then one day, a man named Harold Thorson knocked on my door while my mom and stepdad were at work. He spoke with what looked like a microphone pressed to his throat—it was an electrolarynx—and he invited me and my family to worship at the church he attended.

I attended that first Sunday, met three cute girls, and decided I was interested in getting more involved. I didn't believe in God, but I believed in girls and so I began attending church regularly, and eventually Sunday school and youth group. I ultimately married one of those girls, right out of high school. We just celebrated our fortieth anniversary the year I wrote this book.

But while it was my interest in girls that led me to get more involved in church, it was reading the Gospel of Luke that led me to become a follower of Jesus. That summer of 1978, I decided to read the entire Bible, starting with Genesis. By the time I got to the Psalms I had come to believe in God. And it was as I read the Gospel of Luke and saw its emphasis on Jesus's concern for the lowly, the marginalized, the broken, the picked on and pushed around, that I came to love Jesus. On the night I finished reading Luke, I dropped to my knees next to my bed and prayed, "Jesus, I want to follow you. I'd like to be your disciple. I know I'm just fourteen years old, but if you can use me in any way, I offer my life to you."

My life was changed by reading Luke's account of the life, message, ministry, death, and resurrection of Jesus. That decision to follow him did not end the chaos at home. But it did bring a sense of inner peace, a sense of strength, an awareness of God's care for the broken, the outsiders, the outcasts.

In this book we'll study many of the most loved passages in Luke, passages in which this emphasis on God's concern for the outsiders is front and center, passages that remind us that Jesus, like Garth Brooks, had "friends in low places." As a young man reading this Gospel, I felt in its words that Jesus would befriend me. I hope you feel that as you study this Gospel too.

A Plan for Reading this Book

My hope is that you will read the Gospel of Luke alongside this book. I've put together a 40-day daily reading plan for Luke's Gospel. Each daily reading is less than fifteen minutes. If you are reading this book for Lent, plan to read one chapter of it each week along with the daily Gospel readings for that week. Each chapter will correspond to one of the six weeks of Lent, with the postscript to be read the week after Easter. A copy of this reading plan can be found at www.AdamHamilton.com/Luke.

If you are reading this book with a group of friends, there are short videos I've recorded to go along with each chapter. There will be several thousand churches that will read and study Luke together this Lent, with pastors preaching from Luke, and children, youth and adult study groups studying this book and Luke's Gospel together. You can find resources for children, youth, and adults at www.AdamHamilton.com/Luke.

Authorship, Dating, and Major Themes

Scholarly commentaries on the various books of the Bible typically begin with their own introduction describing what can be known about the book's authorship, date of composition, and major themes. I'll give you a very brief summary of the consensus of mainline scholarship.

One thing to note as you study these questions about any New Testament book is that conservative scholars tend to defend the traditional authorship of the New Testament's books and date the books as early as possible. Secular scholars tend to question the traditional authorship claims of the New Testament books and usually make the case for much later dates. Most mainstream evangelical and mainline scholars land somewhere between the two, supporting traditional authorship in many cases but questioning it in others. Likewise, they'll tend to support early dating in some cases; but, with few exceptions, their dating is later than conservative dates and earlier than secular dates.

When it comes to Luke, conservative scholars accept the traditional claims that Luke, the beloved physician, composed the book sometime as early as the mid-fifties to the early sixties AD. Secular scholars note that the Gospels were all written anonymously, and that Luke's name does not appear in the Gospel. The names Matthew, Mark, Luke, and John were added later based upon church tradition. They often date Luke to near the end of the first century or the first quarter of the second century. Finally, evangelical mainstream and mainline scholars recognize the Gospels are anonymous, with many accepting that Luke, Paul's sometime traveling companion, may have composed the Gospel, while some are less certain. The mainstream evangelical and mainline consensus is that the Gospel of Luke was written between AD 75 and 90.

Let's spend a few more minutes speaking about authorship and then I'll give you a summary of where we're going in the chapters ahead.

Authorship

As noted above, unlike nearly all the letters of the New Testament, none of the New Testament Gospels identify their authors. They are anonymous. But early in church history they became associated with their familiar names: Matthew, Mark, Luke, and John. Matthew and John were apostles, and Mark was believed to have known Jesus. He was a cousin of Barnabas and an early traveling companion of Paul.

While Luke's name appears nowhere in the text of the Gospel or in Acts, he is mentioned by name in Colossians 4:14 where Paul[1] writes of "Luke, the dearly loved physician" in a way that makes clear that he was with Paul while in prison as he wrote Colossians. Many point to the interesting medical details and terminology found in the

Gospel of Luke as being consistent with Colossians 4:14 identifying Luke as a "dearly loved physician."

We also find Luke mentioned in Philemon 24. There Paul mentions his companions who are with him wherever he is imprisoned—perhaps in Caesarea Maritima or in Rome. Paul notes that Luke was among those companions. We read something similar in 2 Timothy 4:11, whose setting is near the end of Paul's life. He is in prison, awaiting execution, and there Paul notes, "Only Luke is with me." These references make clear that Luke was seen by the early church as a faithful traveling companion with Paul and a steadfast friend during Paul's various times of imprisonment.

This idea is consistent with multiple passages in Acts where the author speaks in the first-person plural of Paul's travels. An example of this is Acts 16:11-12 (emphasis added), which begins the "we section" of Acts,

> *We sailed from Troas straight for Samothrace and came to Neapolis the following day. From there **we** went to Philippi, a city of Macedonia's first district and a Roman colony. **We** stayed in that city several days.*

The author's use of "we," many believe, is not accidental, nor is it a literary device, but indicates that the author, presumably Luke, was traveling with Paul for the events described. The early church accepted that this was evidence of Luke and Acts being written by a traveling companion of Paul: the dearly loved physician, Luke. If Luke did indeed write this book, I can't help wondering if some of the material in the book came from Paul himself. Paul seldom quotes Jesus, and even less often refers to stories from his life, but Luke's writing of this Gospel would suggest that Paul knew the Gospel stories as he preached and taught about Jesus. It's been said that Mark's Gospel was shaped by Mark's association with Peter. Perhaps Luke includes much of what Paul knew and preached about Jesus but did not include in his epistles.

To Whom Was Luke Written and Why?

The Gospel of Luke and the Acts of the Apostles were written by the same person and to the same recipient, one "Theophilus"—a name that means "lover of God" or "friend of God." Some believe the name was not that of a person but used to describe anyone who sought to be lovers or friends of God and who were followers of Jesus. If that was the case, then each of us who seeks to know Jesus, or who is already committed to following Jesus, might be Theophilus.

Yet the consensus is that Theophilus was a real person, a person wealthy enough to fund Luke's work in researching and writing the Gospel. This was no small task. Luke tells us he met with eyewitnesses (did he travel to Jerusalem for this?) and acquired copies of other early gospels or pre-gospels in order to write what he hoped would be the most accurate account of the birth, life, teachings, ministry, death, and resurrection of Jesus. The Gospel may have been commissioned by Theophilus, but it was no doubt intended for a much broader audience. Theophilus certainly got his money's worth as, nearly two thousand years later, the Gospel has been read by billions of people throughout history.

Ultimately, we may not know with certainty when Luke was written or even whether the author's name was Luke. What we can know is that the author, presumably Luke, took his job seriously. In the introduction of Luke, a passage you've seen at the opening of this introduction, he wrote,

> **Many people have already applied themselves to the task of compiling an account** of the events that have been fulfilled among us. They used what the **original eyewitnesses** and servants of the word handed down to us. Now, after having **investigated everything carefully** from the beginning, I have also decided to write a carefully ordered account for you, most honorable Theophilus. **I want you to have confidence** in the soundness of the instruction you have received.
>
> (Luke 1:1-4, emphasis added)

Notice that Luke mentions that *many* had already compiled accounts of the story of Jesus. This is fascinating. The only Gospel we know of that is believed to have been written prior to Luke is Mark. So where are these other compilations? It's thought that they are preserved in Luke, Matthew, John, and perhaps even Mark. Each of these Gospel writers had sources available to them, some of which were compilations of Jesus's teachings and stories of his life. Scholars believe that Matthew and Luke had access to Mark. Some suggest that Luke had access to Matthew, or that Matthew had access to Luke (though we might suppose that there would not be so many areas of disagreement between these two Gospels if one relied on the other). More likely, both Matthew and Luke had access to compilations of Jesus's teaching, his miraculous healings, passion narratives and Easter stories, and more. We know that Luke and Matthew both quote Mark, virtually word for word at times. But they also both seem to quote at least one other source, perhaps more.

What is most important to note from Luke's introduction is that he has carefully researched his Gospel and he wants the reader to have confidence in the veracity of what he has written and ultimately in their faith.

Like each of the Gospels, Luke was not merely a biography of Jesus. It was a gospel (which means good news) meant to confirm and deepen the faith of those, like Theophilus, who had already come to believe. It was also meant to persuade those who were interested in or open to hearing the gospel—the good news of Jesus Christ—to become Jesus-followers. Luke sought to paint a compelling picture of Jesus, but this picture of Jesus was particularly compelling to those who identified with Luke's stories.

John tells us at the end of his Gospel that "Jesus did many other things as well. If all of them were recorded, I imagine the world itself wouldn't have enough room for the scrolls that would be written" (John 21:25). Even if John deploys a bit of hyperbole, the point is clear: there were many stories from the life and ministry of Jesus that could have been told. John chose certain ones for his purpose. Luke chose others for his purposes. And what are Luke's purposes? He wants to confirm and give confidence to the faith of those who have come to believe. But he also writes to beckon people to put their faith in Christ. In particular, he seems to want to appeal to the same people he notes Jesus appealed to: the outsiders, the outcasts, and even the outlaws, or, said another way, the marginalized, the broken, the poor and pitiable, and all the people who felt unseen or alone, or second class.

A Brief Outline of What's Ahead

Each chapter in this book will tell the story of Jesus as found in Luke by highlighting some of Jesus's "friends in low places." As we do this, you'll come to see just how important this theme is to Luke. It was this idea that won my heart to Christ, just as I believe Luke intended when he wrote this Gospel. Here's where we're going as we progress through the book:

In chapter 1, we'll turn to the Gospel's opening to see how God chose and used the elderly and infertile, as well as the young, the poor, and the powerless, as we turn to the stories surrounding the birth of John the Baptist and his cousin, Jesus.

In chapter 2, we'll turn to Luke's emphasis on Jesus's ministry with and for women including the demon-possessed Mary of Magdala with the voices in her head, the sinful woman who wept at Jesus's feet, and the conflict between two sisters, Mary and Martha, trying to understand how Jesus saw a woman's role in his ministry.

In chapter 3, we'll consider Jesus's parables and how often in Luke Jesus makes the sinners, the sickly, the tax collectors, and the Samaritans the heroes of his stories, and the religious hypocrites the villains.

In chapter 4, we'll turn to Jesus's final journey to Jerusalem, a journey that takes up nearly half of the Gospel. On this journey, Jesus ministered to Samaritan lepers, a chief tax collector named

Zacchaeus, and others who were outcasts, outsiders, and outlaws to their people, climaxing with his dramatic statement, "the Son of Man came to seek and save the lost" (Luke 19:10 NRSV).

In chapter 5, we'll turn to the events of Holy Week as Jesus entered Jerusalem "humble and riding on a donkey" (Matthew 21:5; see also Zechariah 9:9). There he overturns the tables of the wealthy and powerful merchants in the Temple, praises a poor widow who gave her last "mite" in her offering to God. At the Last Supper, Jesus addresses a debate among his disciples about which one of them was the "greatest."

In chapter 6, we'll turn to the crucifixion of Jesus, and the words Luke records Jesus saying from the cross—words that only appear in Luke's Gospel: from the cross, Jesus prayed for the forgiveness of his abusers, offered salvation to an outlaw, and then entrusted his life into his Father's hands.

Finally, in the postscript, we'll turn to the Resurrection and the meaning of this powerful event, particularly for all who have struggled and felt powerless. We'll see, in keeping with Luke's theme, who Jesus chooses to be the first witnesses to the Resurrection and to help his readers see how the Resurrection speaks to them.

It was reading this Gospel when I was fourteen—this Gospel for the outsiders, the outcasts, and the outlaws—that I fell in love with Jesus and decided to commit my life to him. My hope is that in studying this Gospel, if you are not yet a Christian, you might hear the good news of Jesus and decide, as I did, you want to follow Jesus and be his disciple. And if you are already a follower of Jesus, I hope your faith grows deeper, and your commitment stronger, as you seek to embody his life and teachings, his death and resurrection, in your life.

I'd love to invite you to join me in this prayer,

Lord, as I begin this study of Luke's Gospel, open my ears to hear, and my heart to receive, all that you want to say to me. Help me to see you, to hear you, and ultimately to follow you. Amen.

1

LIFTING UP THE LOWLY

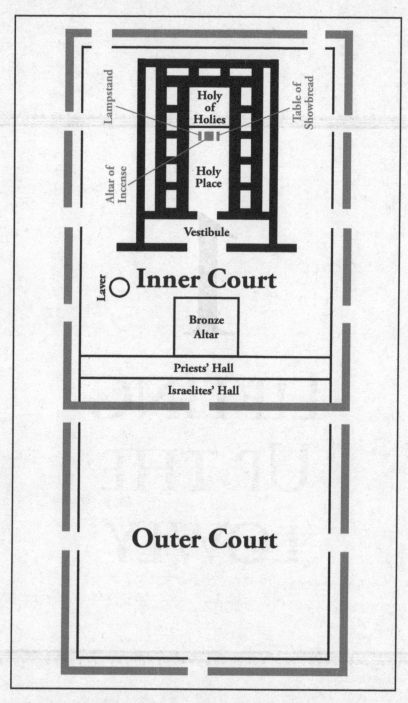

Lampstand

Table of Showbread

Holy of Holies

Altar of Incense

Holy Place

Vestibule

Laver

Inner Court

Bronze Altar

Priests' Hall

Israelites' Hall

Outer Court

A diagram of the Temple in Jerusalem. The angel Gabriel appeared to Zechariah beside the incense altar in the Holy Place (Luke 1:5-25). Simeon and Anna encountered the infant Jesus in the "temple area," most likely in the outer court (Luke 2:25-38).

1

LIFTING UP
THE LOWLY

He has shown strength with his arm.
    He has scattered those with arrogant thoughts and proud
      inclinations.
    He has pulled the powerful down from their thrones
      and lifted up the lowly.
He has filled the hungry with good things
    and sent the rich away empty-handed.

                                          (Luke 1:51-53)

"Line up!" our gym teacher shouted. "It's time to divide teams for kickball." I was not particularly good at kickball in third grade. I don't know if it was a clumsy phase, or my poor hand-eye coordination, or that I was afraid of getting hit by the ball, but even at eight it was clear I was never going to make the world kickball championship team (yes, there are national championship teams in kickball!). I didn't mind not being great at kickball. What I hated was when we divided up the teams.

There were two kids who were regularly chosen to be captains. They were taller, stronger, more athletic, and cooler than the rest of us. They would go back and forth choosing who they wanted on their team. And I'd stand there, a skinny orange-haired kid who hadn't had a growth spurt yet, a bit awkward in my own skin, hoping and praying that someone would pick me. That was a year of repeated

3

humiliation when, on multiple occasions, I was the last kid chosen, the kid one team was forced to take.

Now imagine a team captain who looked at the potential players, and her first choice was the scrawny, awkward kids that no one wanted. And with each successive choice she chose the next worst player. She'd have the "Bad News Bears" of kickball, a group of utterly unlikely candidates who were certain to be a losing team, but who, in the end, became the championship team.

In a sense, this is how Luke sees the gospel, and God's character and kingdom as well as the driving passion of Jesus's ministry, the purpose of his crucifixion, and the victory achieved in his resurrection. Some have called Luke's emphasis "the great reversal." You can see it on nearly every page of Luke's Gospel. Let's begin our study where Luke begins, with the Annunciation and Nativity stories of John the Baptist and Jesus.

They Were Both Very Old

During the rule of King Herod of Judea there was a priest named Zechariah who belonged to the priestly division of Abijah. His wife Elizabeth was a descendant of Aaron. They were both righteous before God, blameless in their observance of all the Lord's commandments and regulations. They had no children because Elizabeth was unable to become pregnant and they both were very old.

(Luke 1:5-7)

With these words, Luke formally begins his account of the Gospel of Jesus by telling us the story of John the Baptist's parents. No other Gospel, in fact no other New Testament book, mentions Elizabeth and Zechariah. I devote a great deal of time unpacking this story in my last book, *Prepare the Way for the Lord: Advent and the Message of John the Baptist* (Abingdon, 2022). Here, I'll only briefly touch on a few of the details Luke wants us to notice as he introduces his theme concerning the unlikely people God favors and chooses to use.

Notice that Luke tells us Elizabeth and Zechariah were righteous before God, yet "they had no children because Elizabeth was unable to become pregnant." And he adds "and they both were very old."

The elderly held a place of honor in first-century Judaism. Younger adults were to stand when someone over sixty walked into the room. But it was likely that ageism toward older adults was present then as today. In our hurry-up lives, when we get behind someone who is driving slowly, we say they are "driving like a grandpa." When we are hiring people for a job, we don't tend to start with seasoned candidates with a lifetime of experience, people in their sixties or even their fifties. Employers are looking for someone in their thirties. In a recent national study, 80 percent of adults fifty to eighty indicate they have experienced some form of age discrimination.

Among the most overt and visible places for age discrimination is in news and entertainment. There is a recognized double standard where leading male actors and anchorpersons are routinely ten years or more older than their female counterparts. There have been numerous lawsuits filed by female anchorpersons who were released from their jobs, or taken off the air, as they aged. One award-winning female anchorwoman who was replaced with a woman ten years younger offered this advice: "Whatever you do, don't get old."[1]

The church world is not immune to this. It has been a standing joke among clergy for years that the average local church has an ideal pastor for their congregation: male, thirty-five years old, with two-point-five children. And, unless the congregation is made up of people of color, the unnamed criterion is usually white. The joke didn't seem so offensive when I was in my thirties, but today it's not so funny. The challenge is not just felt by pastors, but by worship leaders and a host of other staff. This tendency to devalue adults over sixty is felt by parishioners in many congregations as well, who sometimes feel that in the churches they've attended for decades, they are now "the last ones picked for the team."

But Luke's Gospel starts with God choosing the "very old" Elizabeth and Zechariah to give birth to the prophet who would prepare the way for the Messiah. Elizabeth and Zechariah are not the only examples of this in the Gospel. If you have your Bible, turn to Luke 2:25 where Mary and Joseph bring Jesus to the Temple. A man named Simeon, grateful to have seen the child, prays that God can now take him for he had "seen your salvation." Simeon would seem to be an older man. Next, consider Anna, beginning in Luke 2:36:

> *There was also a prophet, Anna the daughter of Phanuel, who belonged to the tribe of Asher. She was very old. After she married, she lived with her husband for seven years. She was now an 84-year-old widow. She never left the temple area but worshipped God with fasting and prayer night and day. She approached at that very moment and began to praise God and to speak about Jesus to everyone who was looking forward to the redemption of Jerusalem.*
>
> *(Luke 2:36-38)*

God chose the least likely couple in the world to produce a nation that would be God's special covenant people.

In each case, there are older adults, people largely sidelined by society then as now, whom God chose and used. This is nothing new to Luke. God called Abraham and Sarah, at the age of seventy-five and sixty-five, respectively, to leave all that was familiar to them and move to the Promised Land. Sarah was ninety and Abraham a hundred when God finally blessed this infertile couple with a child, Isaac. Now, I'd prefer not to experience this latter blessing of a child at one hundred, but the point is that God chose the least likely couple in the world to produce a nation that would be God's special covenant people. Moses was eighty when he led the children of Israel out of slavery in Egypt. Again and again God chooses and uses those who are "over the hill" to accomplish his greatest purposes. God's affection for the aging is captured well in Isaiah:

> *Even to your old age and gray hairs*
> *I am he, I am he who will sustain you.*
> *I have made you and I will carry you;*
> *I will sustain you and I will rescue you.*
>
> *(Isaiah 46:4 NIV)*

A Lifelong Struggle with Infertility

Notice Elizabeth and Zechariah were not just an older couple, but a couple who had struggled with infertility. They had prayed and prayed and prayed to have a child but had never been able to conceive. This was considered by many at the time to be a sign that God did not favor a woman—a source of shame and disgrace in a time when infertility was not understood. Even today, I've known many couples, particularly the woman trying to conceive, who experience infertility as a source of great pain. Many wonder where God is in the midst of their heartache.

Scripture does not see infertility as a sign of God's displeasure or disregard, but often those struggling with infertility may believe it does. Today, we understand many of the physiological causes of infertility and don't see this as an act of God.

But throughout the Bible we do find God's compassion and concern for those who wrestled with infertility. And often, when some special part of God's story needed a child to be born, it was couples who had struggled with infertility that God chose for the task. In the Old Testament, God chose Abraham and Sarah, Isaac and Rebekah, Jacob and Rachel, and Hannah and Elkanah, each an infertile couple, for a special role in his plans.

Nevertheless, in the first-century setting of this story, God's choice of this elderly couple who had known the pain of infertility is another example of God's compassion and God's choosing and using the outsider, for that is what Elizabeth's infertility left her feeling. We can both see and feel that in Elizabeth's words after she conceived, "This is the Lord's doing. He has shown his favor to me *by removing my disgrace among other people*" (Luke 1:25, emphasis added).

Hitting Your Stride?

From the opening chapters of Luke, the Gospel writer shows us God's choice of those who are older. Our society often values the nimbleness and energy of youth and undervalues the wisdom and knowledge of those who are older.

Harvard professor Arthur Brooks recently wrote a book titled *From Strength to Strength* about finding purpose, meaning, and success as we age. The premise is important and familiar to many of us: the skills, intelligence, and abilities that can lead to certain kinds of success in the first half of our lives and careers will not continue undiminished throughout our lives.

Think of Tom Brady, the superstar NFL quarterback who won his *seventh* Super Bowl in 2021 at the age of forty-three. In his twenties and early thirties, Brady was fast, agile, strong, and quick to make decisions. These skills of his diminished over time, as they do for all of us. In his later thirties and early forties, however, different strengths began to emerge. What Brady came to count on was not speed or strength or quickness of thought, but twenty-two years of experience, wisdom, and knowledge of the game.

Brooks doesn't speak about Tom Brady in his book, but he does describe two kinds of intelligence that I think Tom Brady illustrates. Brooks speaks of *fluid intelligence* and *crystallized intelligence*. As one declines, the other continues to grow and expand. Fluid intelligence includes problem solving, quickness of thought, memory, adaptation, pliability. Its physical corollaries are strength, speed, and the ability to work seventy hours a week.

As fluid intelligence starts to diminish, crystallized intelligence emerges and grows. Crystallized intelligence is the vast body of knowledge you have that continues to grow. It is maturity, wisdom, insight, experience. We see all of this in the Christian spiritual life as well. As we age, we have the potential to have more patience, grace, humility, love, understanding, knowledge, wisdom.

A midlife crisis often comes as we recognize the unmistakable decline of our fluid intelligence. We also find that the world can sometimes miss out on seeing the value of crystallized intelligence and all that goes with aging. We can "put people out to pasture" or consider them "all washed up." It's important to value youth, but we can so value youth that we miss out on the gifts of age.

The Tampa Bay Buccaneers recognized an opportunity in signing Tom Brady. Most of his career was behind him, but he might play a couple of years for them. Crucially, they realized that he could more than make up for his lack of fluid intelligence with his high crystallized intelligence. He still had the gifts to win a Super Bowl for them. Perhaps even more importantly, he would also pass on his wisdom and knowledge—his crystallized intelligence—to an entire team of younger players.

There are fields where crystallized intelligence is prized and essential. We don't allow people to run for president of the United States before the age of thirty-five. We feel a position this important needs a certain level of wisdom, and we don't elect people until they are capable of having a fair amount of crystallized intelligence. College professors tend to be more valued the longer they've been researching, writing, and teaching—most get better with age. Doctors are valued in so many ways the more experience they have. The same is true of football coaches. The average age of an NFL head coach is forty-nine. Andy Reid, coach of the Kansas City Chiefs, is sixty-four as I'm writing this book. His last five years have been his best years ever as an NFL head coach.

I think this is part of why God so frequently chooses older adults in scripture. I think God often chooses people who have the humility to say "It's not about me," who have gained a lifetime of wisdom, and who have put their trust in God.

When we reach the point in life where crystallized intelligence surpasses fluid intelligence, we should be thinking about how we can use our crystallized knowledge to have the greatest possible impact. Many, at this point, consider launching a new career in the ministry. Any guess what is the average age of a seminary student? It's right around forty. While you'll find students who are twenty-two, fresh out of college, you'll also find students who are in their sixties. In fact, one Resurrection member who is sixty recently started seminary.

God often chooses and uses people the world might see as "over the hill" to do God's greatest work. I see it every day at the church I serve. Older adults provide most of our volunteers in nearly every ministry area. They pack backpacks to relieve hunger each week. They chair many of our committees. They coordinate our mission trips, lead Bible studies, teach children, and mentor others. They sing in the choir, drive and operate our mobile food pantry, our book mobile, and our furnishings truck. The church could not survive were it not for the older adults who give such great leadership. At Resurrection we require that all our leadership teams be comprised of one-third people over fifty-five, one-third people thirty-five to fifty-five, and one-third people fifteen to thirty-five. Why? Because we need the leadership and mentoring of those who are over fifty-five, and the perspective, energy, and passion of those under thirty-five, and everyone in between.

If you are an older adult, God is not finished with you yet. It may be your most productive, influential, and fruitful years are all ahead of you. The most important, meaningful, and joyful years in Elizabeth and Zechariah's lives all occurred when they were "very old."

God Chooses and Uses Young Adults

Luke 1–2 also points out that God chooses and uses young people, preteens, and young teens—people who in the first-century world had not yet earned the respect or right to be heard. Mary was engaged to Joseph, a carpenter and handyman[2] from Nazareth. Girls were typically married shortly after their first period, around age fourteen, perhaps younger. After the annunciation to Zechariah and Elizabeth, Luke shifts to thirteen- or fourteen-year-old Mary, to whom the angel Gabriel appears one day in her town of Nazareth saying, "Rejoice, favored one! The Lord is with you!" (Luke 1:28).

Mary was understandably perplexed! Read to what happens next:

The angel said, "Don't be afraid, Mary. God is honoring you. Look! You will conceive and give birth to a son, and you will name him Jesus. He will be great and he will be called the Son of the Most High. The Lord God will give him the throne of David his father. He will rule over Jacob's house forever, and there will be no end to his kingdom."

Then Mary said to the angel, "How will this happen since I haven't had sexual relations with a man?"

The angel replied, "The Holy Spirit will come over you and the power of the Most High will overshadow you. Therefore, the one who is to be born will be holy. He will be called God's Son. Look, even in her old age, your relative Elizabeth has conceived a son. This woman who was labeled 'unable to conceive' is now six months pregnant. Nothing is impossible for God."

(Luke 1:30-37)

For the single most significant event that will happen on earth since creation, the Incarnation—God coming to us, as one of us, to save, deliver, and redeem the human race—God chose to use a thirteen- or fourteen-year-old girl from an insignificant family who lived on the "other side of the tracks."

I often remind our confirmation class at Resurrection that Mary was their age when she was chosen by God for this important task. I remind them that God chooses and uses young adults *throughout* scripture, people in their teens and twenties. David was just a boy when he fought Goliath, the giant Philistine. It was the young princess Esther who worked up the courage to save the Jewish people from genocide. It was Timothy whom Paul left to pastor in Ephesus, to whom Paul would write, "Don't let anyone look down on you because you are young. Instead, set an example for the believers through your speech, behavior, love, faith, and by being sexually pure" (1 Timothy 4:12).

Paul's words to Timothy illustrate an attitude we sometimes see toward people who are young: older people might look down upon them, dismiss them, patronize them, or fail to take them seriously because of their youth. We might think a young person hasn't lived long enough, hasn't learned enough, hasn't experienced enough to lead or contribute meaningfully. Ageism works in both directions. But Luke's account of Mary, as well as the other stories of young people in scripture, shows that God chooses and uses those whom others might regard as "too young."

I felt called to be a pastor when I was sixteen, but there are many who first hear the call to be in ministry before that. Anna Sarol is a member of Resurrection who was paralyzed from the waist down in a tragic gymnastics accident when she was fourteen. Out of that tragedy, she focused on what God could do with her life. She said, "I never thought, 'Why me?' I knew I had a bigger purpose: to use this pain and all these hard times. I hope to inspire other people's lives and show them I'm still smiling." Anna is amazing. She speaks to schools, advocating for persons with disabilities and encouraging people who are facing struggles. She uses social media to encourage and lift others up. She also serves on our church council, our senior leadership team at Resurrection. God uses her in profound ways. She feels called to a life of service, either in medicine or some other field.

Anna felt called at the age of fourteen, out of her tragedy, to use her experience to minister to and encourage others. Do a Google search of her and you'll find video clips and stories about this amazing young woman.

When you feel God calling you to do something that requires courage, or sacrifice, or faithfulness, join in Mary's words, "I am the Lord's servant. Let it be with me just as you have said."

When God called Mary at the age of thirteen or fourteen to this frightening task that would be filled with challenges and joy, a task that would end in pain as she watched her son die, this was her response: "I am the Lord's servant. Let it be with me just as you have said" (Luke 1:38). Mary's words reflect a prayer I've taught our congregation to pray. When you feel God calling you to do something that requires courage, or sacrifice, or faithfulness, join in Mary's words, "I am the Lord's servant. Let it be with me just as you have said." When, in the midst of a sermon or while reading scripture, you sense the gentle nudge of the Holy Spirit or the urgent plea for help, may you say with Mary, "I am the Lord's servant. Let it be with me just as you have said." Would you pause right now to pray these words aloud to God: "I am the Lord's servant. Let it be with me just as you have said."

Whether you are very young, very old, or somewhere in between, I hope that Mary's words would come freely to your lips, and to my lips, and as they do, you'll find that God uses you to accomplish his purposes no matter how unlikely a candidate you might be.

God Lifts Up the Lowly

That leads me to Mary's powerful hymn, the Magnificat. Immediately after Mary discovered she was pregnant, she went to find her older cousin, or perhaps aunt, Elizabeth. Elizabeth is, by now, in her sixth month of pregnancy. Elizabeth was an older mentor to Mary.[3] And upon hearing Elizabeth bless her, Mary shouts the beautiful words of the Magnificat. I want you to notice, in particular, the words in plain type:

> *"With all my heart I glorify the Lord!*
>   *In the depths of who I am I rejoice in God my savior.*
> *He has **looked with favor on the low status of his servant.***
>   *Look! From now on, everyone will consider me highly favored*
>   *because the mighty one has done great things for me.*
> *Holy is his name.*
>   *He shows mercy to everyone,*
>   *from one generation to the next,*
>   *who honors him as God.*
> *He has shown strength with his arm.*
>   *He has scattered those with arrogant thoughts and proud*
>   *inclinations.*
> ***He has pulled the powerful down from their thrones***
>   ***and lifted up the lowly.***
> ***He has filled the hungry with good things***
>   ***and sent the rich away empty-handed.***
>   *(Luke 1:46-53, emphasis added)*

It is on the lips of Mary that Luke lays out the theme of his Gospel, the theme of this book: God looks with favor on those of low status. God brings down the powerful from their thrones. *God lifts up the lowly.* God chooses the people others think are washed up or have no value. God values and uses those who have been pushed down, oppressed, or disdained. This one line captures Luke's theme. Read it aloud with me, *"God lifts up the lowly."* But *who* are the lowly, and *how* does God lift them up?

The *'Am ha-Arez*

Let's start with the who. The Greek and Hebrew words for lowly both signify humility, of a humble state, but also those whom others consider lowly, or who have been pushed down by others. This includes the poor, the powerless, and those who struggled with a variety of physical and mental illnesses. It could be the uneducated as well as the religiously unobservant—the nonreligious or nominally religious people of the day—as well as those others considered sinners.

In Hebrew the phrase *'Am ha-Arez*—"the people of the land"—was often used for many of these types of people. It was a condescending and derogatory phrase that the educated, sophisticated, wealthy, and religiously devout used to describe those who were none of these things. They used it in the sense that someone might use the word *bumpkin* today, or *ignoramus*. It meant vulgar, uncouth, uneducated. It was used of the masses of people who did not show up at synagogue, or who did not observe all the laws and rules the religious leaders taught. The online *Jewish Encyclopedia* notes that by the first century, "the faithful observers of the law (Pharisees) shunned any contact with an 'Am ha-Arez."[4]

These *'Am ha-Arez* included most of the people Luke describes Jesus ministering with. As we will see, he is constantly lifting up these lowly. While Mary was undoubtedly religiously devout, because of her standing in society, a servant girl from the no-account village of Nazareth, she, too, may have been seen as an *'Am ha-Arez* in the sense of a "bumpkin," lacking sophistication and appearing uncouth.

God, in choosing her, has lifted up the lowly. Mary's son will devote his ministry to doing the same for the *'Am ha-Arez* he encounters. Interestingly, the *Jewish Encyclopedia* notes,

> There can be no doubt that it was this contemptuous and hostile attitude of the Pharisaic schools toward the masses that was the chief cause of the triumphant power

of the Christian church. In preaching the good tidings to the poor and the out-cast, Jesus of Nazareth won the great masses of Judea. The Pharisaic schools, laying all stress on the Law and on learning, held the 'Am ha-Arez in utter contempt. The new Christian sect recruited itself chiefly from the ranks of the untaught, laying special stress on the merits of the simple and the humble.[5]

The paragraph above was a Jewish scholar's assessment of the appeal of the Christian faith in the first century. Luke's Gospel is a chief champion for this emphasis of the Christian gospel.

How Does God Lift Up the Lowly?

While God directly lifts up Mary, the Gospel focuses on Jesus's work of lifting up the lowly. But following Jesus's death and resurrection, he passes this calling on to us. We are called to lift up the lowly as we seek to follow Christ. The church, Paul tells us, is the "body of Christ"—we continue to incarnate his presence. We continue to pursue his work of lifting up the lowly. And there is something in us followers of Christ that compels us to do this work.

In February 2022, Russia's president, Vladimir Putin, sent troops to invade Ukraine under false pretenses. Many of us were stunned to watch, in real time, as one of the most powerful nations on earth sent tanks and fighter planes and missile batteries to wage war against a neighbor who had done nothing to provoke the attack, a neighbor who was far weaker.

Ukraine heroically sought to resist and repel the Russians. As we watched these events, most were inspired by Ukrainian president Volodymyr Zelensky and the Ukrainian people. We found ourselves tying ribbons around our trees, sending aid, supporting military assistance, giving millions of dollars to stand with the Ukrainians. Why? Because we were created in the image of a God whose nature is to lift up the lowly and to stand against bullies.

Hear Mary's words again: *He has pulled the powerful down from their thrones and lifted up the lowly.* As I write these words, I still don't know how this conflict will end. What I know is that, in a sense, President Putin has already lost. He has become a pariah in the world's eyes. Countries that never thought about joining NATO are now contemplating it. He is weakened as a global leader. And I am certain that one day, in some way, he will find himself brought down from his throne.

He has pulled the powerful down from their thrones and lifted up the lowly.

How does God lift up the lowly and send the hungry away with food? He does it by moving our hearts and calling his people to help. But this only works when we say, with Mary, "I am the Lord's servant. Let it be with me just as you have said."

During the opening months of this war, I traveled with a small team to the border between Poland and Ukraine. Three million refugees crossed the border into Poland and beyond. We saw the aid tents, visited the temporary shelters, and met some of these refugees, listening to their stories. We communicated our concern and care for them, and God's care for them. We came back with a clear idea how our congregation and others could "lift up the lowly," sending significant amounts of aid so that the hungry would "be filled with good things."

O Holy Night

I'd like to end this chapter with Luke's telling of the Christmas story. The story of the birth of Jesus appears in Matthew and Luke's Gospels. But their telling of the story is so very different, and in the differences, you can hear Luke's emphasis on God lifting up the lowly and befriending the outsiders.

In Matthew, there is no census by Caesar Augustus, no holy family unable to find a room in the "inn," no birth in a stable, no manger for a crib, no night-shift shepherds. Matthew only mentions a home where the wealthy wise men find the Holy Family, bringing their gifts of gold, frankincense, and myrrh to them.

In Luke, we see the lowliness of Jesus from his birth. He was born to a carpenter-handyman and a peasant girl, forced by a census to travel days before the child's birth. Upon arriving they find there is no place for Mary to give birth, and they are forced to give birth in a stable where the animals slept. For Christ's bed there was an animal's feeding trough—a manger. Luke mentions the manger three times in the story as if to say, "Notice how lowly the circumstances of his birth!" In Luke, it is not wise men, but night-shift shepherds whom God invites to welcome the Christ Child. Shepherds were the epitome of the 'Am ha-Arez that Jesus came to reach. They were typically uneducated, uncouth, and considered among the lowly.

That night that Jesus was born, as the shepherds came to see the Child lying in a manger, he had already begun to lift up the lowly, to befriend the outsiders and outcasts, and to draw them to his Father. As we turn to the rest of the Gospel, we'll find this theme again and again.

Are you "very old"? Good! God is choosing you! Are you too young to be taken seriously by others? Terrific, you are exactly the kind of person God chooses for his team! Have you struggled in life, been rejected by others, known your share of humiliation? Jesus wants to use you. Conversely, are you among the powerful, the wealthy, the revered? God loves and wants you too. "Humble yourself in the sight of the Lord," knowing that God longs to use your power, influence, and resources to lift up the lowly.

2

SIMON,
DO YOU
SEE THIS
WOMAN?

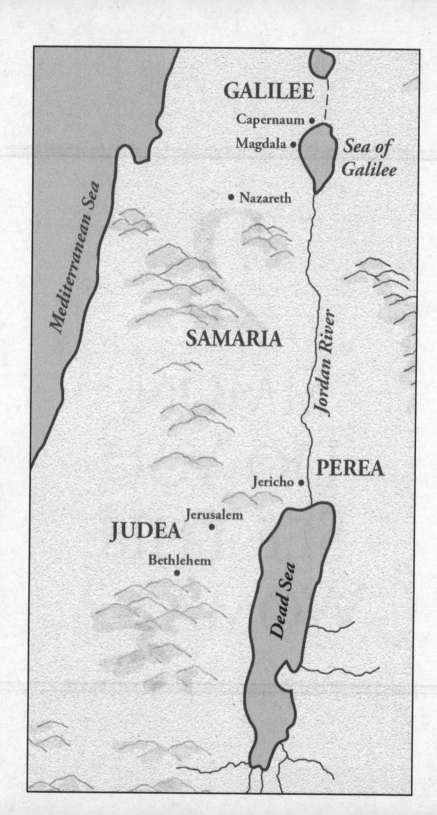

2

SIMON, DO YOU SEE THIS WOMAN?

One of the Pharisees invited Jesus to eat with him. After he entered the Pharisee's home, he took his place at the table. Meanwhile, a woman from the city, a sinner, discovered that Jesus was dining in the Pharisee's house. She brought perfumed oil in a vase made of alabaster. Standing behind him at his feet and crying, she began to wet his feet with her tears. She wiped them with her hair, kissed them, and poured the oil on them. When the Pharisee who had invited Jesus saw what was happening, he said to himself, If this man were a prophet, he would know what kind of woman is touching him. He would know that she is a sinner.

(Luke 7:36-39)

Jesus traveled through the cities and villages, preaching and proclaiming the good news of God's kingdom. The Twelve were with him, along with some women who had been healed of evil spirits and sicknesses. Among them were Mary Magdalene (from whom seven demons had been thrown out), Joanna (the wife of Herod's servant Chuza), Susanna, and many others who provided for them out of their resources.

(Luke 8:1-3)

I recently learned that my granddaughter Stella was born on International Women's Day. It's a day I was not familiar with as it has not been widely observed in the US until recently, but it is observed in a host of countries, celebrating the achievements and

21

efforts of women, advocating for equality for women, and striving to prevent violence and harassment against women. Learning this, as we celebrated Stella's birthday, made me think about the kind of world I want her to grow up in.

I love this little girl more than my own life. I pray for her every day. I want her to know that she is loved by her family and loved by God. I also want her to grow up in a world where women are valued, treated with equity, and where she lives without fear of sexual harassment or sexual violence.

As a nation the US has come a long way since 1919, the year before the 19th Amendment passed, extending the right to vote to women. But recent data from the Department of Labor and the Pew Research Center show that women still make between 80 percent and 84 percent of what a man makes for the same job.[1] Only nine top executives of Fortune 500 companies are women. As I write this book, only 24 percent of the US Senate and 29 percent of the US House of Representatives are women. And in the denomination of which I am a part, The United Methodist Church, only 5 percent of the senior pastors of the largest churches are women.

Regarding violence and harassment against women, the United Nations reports that 741 million women around the world have been victims of some kind of violence, usually at the hands of a spouse or boyfriend. In the United States, one out of every six women experience either attempted or completed sexual assault—that is over 463,000 women in the US every year.[2] In a recent national survey of 2,009 Americans, eighty-one percent of women reported that they had been sexually harassed at some time in their lives.[3]

In this chapter, we'll focus on the ministry of Jesus as it related to women, who were often unseen and devalued in the world in which he lived and ministered. We'll see that Luke, more than any other book of the New Testament, wants his readers to know that Jesus valued women, saw them, had compassion for them, ministered with them, and lifted them up.

The Role of Women
in the Ancient World

Let's begin by considering attitudes toward women in ancient Judaism. One commentator noted of the place of women in ancient Judaism, "Women were considered important only to the extent that they impacted the lives of men."[4] Philo of Alexandria, a Jewish philosopher who lived during the time of Christ, once wrote, "The minds of women are, in some degree, weaker than those of men, and are not so well able to comprehend a thing which is appreciable only by the intellect."[5] The first-century Jewish historian Josephus wrote, regarding the courts, "Let not the testimony of women be admitted."[6] He believed women could not be credible witnesses. A first-century Jewish blessing, to be offered each morning by Jewish men, began, "Blessed are you, Lord our God, Ruler of the Universe, who has not made me a woman." It is still prayed by some Jewish men today. Some first-century rabbis held that women were not to be taught the Torah, for they would misuse and twist it into evil.[7] Women were not allowed to be rabbis, or priests, or elders in the synagogue. Note that this does not mean women and daughters were unloved. But there was no sense in which they were considered equal with men. This was not, of course, only an issue in Judaism. It was true in the Greco-Roman world and nearly everywhere else in the ancient world as well.

We find this attitude toward women reflected in scripture. There are, by some counts, 1,700 unique people mentioned by name in the Bible. Of those, 1,563 are men and only 137 are women. For every one woman who was mentioned by name in scripture, there are eleven men. This represents the patriarchal world of the Bible.

It's customary in United Methodist and other mainline churches to give a child a Bible when they reach the third grade. I remember when I gave our youngest daughter, Rebecca, her Bible when she was eight. I encouraged her to read the Bible each night, and then we would talk about the chapter she read as I put her to bed. She eventually started asking me questions. "Daddy, why don't the girls have names?" And "Daddy, why do the boys get all the best parts?" And "Daddy, how come the boys are sometimes mean to the girls?" She asked those questions just reading through the book of Genesis. I finally said, "Becca, how about we skip ahead to the Gospel of Luke?"

Luke mentions women by name more often than all of the other Gospels.

Luke mentions women by name more often than any of the other Gospels. The book recounts more stories about women. Women speak more lines in Luke than in the other Gospels. There is a pattern in Luke where Luke tells a story involving a man, followed shortly by a similar story involving a woman as he seeks to balance his narrative with both men and women. Women are involved in Jesus's ministry, encouraged to join the men in hearing the word. They are shown dignity and honored and play pivotal roles throughout the Gospel. Let's take a look at a few of the many passages in Luke involving women.

Women in Luke

As we saw in the last chapter, the Gospel of Luke begins by highlighting the stories and voices of Elizabeth and Mary. In Luke 1:41-45, Elizabeth is filled with the Holy Spirit, prophesies over Mary, and becomes the first person in the Gospel to pronounce that Mary's child is the Lord. This is followed by the eighty-four-year-old prophetess Anna, likewise prophesying over the child as the Holy Family dedicated Jesus at the Temple (2:36-38).

If you have your Bible with you, turn to Luke 4:38-39, where, among the first miracles Jesus performs, he heals Simon Peter's mother-in-law of a fever. Turn to Luke 7:11-16. There Jesus sees a funeral procession for a young man, and he sees the boy's mother grieving. Filled with compassion for her, Jesus stops and raises her son from the dead. In the next chapter, Luke 8:40-56, Jesus heals a twelve-year-old daughter of the leader of the local synagogue. As he was on the way, a woman who had suffered from internal hemorrhaging for twelve years reached out and touched the hem of his robe, and she was healed. Skip ahead to Luke 13:10-17, where Jesus heals a woman in the synagogue who had been disabled for eighteen years. He touches her and she is instantly made well. Luke tells us that women were at the Crucifixion in 23:27-29 and in 24:1-10 reports that women were the first to learn of the Resurrection. They became the first to proclaim the resurrection of Jesus to others.

Some of these stories occur in other Gospels as well, but we find them given special attention in Luke's Gospel. Luke, it seems, wants to highlight the way Jesus valued and ministered with women.

I want to focus your attention on Luke 8:1-3 for a moment.

Jesus traveled through the cities and villages, preaching and pro-claiming the good news of God's kingdom. The Twelve were with him, along with some women who had been healed of evil spirits and sicknesses. Among them were Mary Magdalene (from whom seven demons had been thrown out), Joanna (the wife of Herod's servant Chuza), Susanna, and many others who provided for them out of their resources.

This is an important passage. We know the twelve male disciples traveled with Jesus in ministry, but here Luke tells us that there were women who traveled with Jesus too. In the first century, only men were given the title *disciple*, but here these women were, like the twelve male disciples, following Jesus as he traveled, listening to his teaching, undoubtedly assisting with his ministry as Jesus healed

25

the sick, fed the multitudes, and proclaimed the good news of the Kingdom. But Luke specifically tells us that they "provided for them out of their resources." What a remarkable line—that these women made possible the ministry of Jesus by providing funds for him and the disciples to do their work.

Luke tells us that these women had been among those that Jesus healed of evil spirits and sicknesses. He names three of these women, Mary Magdalene, Joanna, and Susanna, but there were clearly others. We know nothing more of Susanna in scripture, a name that appears nowhere else in the New Testament. Joanna is identified as the wife of Chuza. Luke calls him Herod Antipas's servant. The Greek word for servant here is *epitrou*, which is not just a servant, but one who has authority and acts as a steward for Herod. This suggests Joanna was a person of some status, power, and means. She must have had great courage to travel as a disciple of Jesus, supporting him, given that Herod Antipas had executed John the Baptist, and, as we'll see in Luke 23, would mock Jesus by dressing him in royal robes before sending him to Pilate for crucifixion.

First in the list of these female disciples is Mary Magdalene. Mary is a fascinating woman even with the little we know about her in the Gospels. Typically, women were identified in relationship to a man (as with Joanna the wife of Chuza). But Mary is not identified with a husband or father. She is identified with a place, Magdala, on the northwest shore of the Sea of Galilee. Luke also tells us that she had seven demons cast out of her (presumably by Jesus). Regardless of whether we see these demons as literal evil spirits or as the way first-century Jews explained mental or physical illness (schizophrenia, depression, addiction, anxiety, and others), Mary Magdalene's condition must have been dramatic. She had been a deeply troubled woman who had experienced great suffering, a prisoner to these demons. Despite her maladies, either through hard work or inheritance, she amassed enough means to travel with and support Jesus and the disciples.

As we've learned, young women in first-century Judaism were typically married shortly after their first period. I've wondered if Mary had been married, but the demons that afflicted her led also to her being rejected by her husband(s). I've wondered if her demon possession may have been occasioned by pain she'd experienced in her childhood, perhaps some form of child or sexual abuse. We can't know, but we can know that she was likely one who both suffered much and was an outsider or outcast. Jesus set her free of the pain, the voices in her head, the brokenness. He made her whole. And she, in turn, followed and supported him.

Mary Magdalene is recorded in the Gospels as present at the Crucifixion and at Christ's burial, and to have gone, with other women, to the tomb on Easter morning. She is the first to have learned the tomb was empty. She heard from an angel that Christ had been raised. She is the first person to have seen Jesus after his resurrection. She is the first to have proclaimed Jesus was raised from the dead. She plays a central place in Jesus's ministry.

The last few years have seen fundamentalist Christians debating whether women can teach, preach, and lead churches given Paul's words, "Let a woman learn in silence with full submission. I permit no woman to teach or to have authority over a man; she is to keep silent" (1 Timothy 2:11-12 NRSV). Yet when we look at the ministry of Jesus, the women who supported him and acted as disciples, and Mary Magdalene in particular, who was the first witness to the Resurrection, we get a different picture, not of Jesus silencing women, but of his calling and empowering them.

As we learned in the introduction, Luke tells us that he had various sources he drew from as he wrote his Gospel, including those who were eyewitnesses. We learned that Luke has material in his Gospel that does not appear in any other Gospel. Some scholars have suggested that the unique material in Luke may have come from the female disciples of Jesus. Some of what we find in Luke that is not in Matthew or Mark are the stories about women or that emphasize Jesus's ministry with women. These stories would have been important to, and remembered by, Mary Magdalene, Joanna, Susanna, and others. There is no way we can know for sure who was the source of this unique material in Luke, but it is an intriguing possibility that women first shared and passed down a good portion of the unique material we find in Luke.

Mary and Martha

Let's take a look at one of the memorable stories that only appears in Luke's Gospel, related to two additional female disciples of Jesus. Here is the account in Luke 10:38-42:

> While Jesus and his disciples were traveling, Jesus entered a village where a woman named Martha welcomed him as a guest. She had a sister named Mary, who sat at the Lord's feet and listened to his message. By contrast, Martha was preoccupied with getting everything ready for their meal. So Martha came to him and said, "Lord, don't you care that my sister has left me to prepare the table all by myself? Tell her to help me."
>
> The Lord answered, "Martha, Martha, you are worried and distracted by many things. One thing is necessary. Mary has chosen the better part. It won't be taken away from her."

Part of why so many love this story is that we can easily see ourselves in Martha or Mary. Close attention to the details of the passage shows us even more. First, this story follows the parable of the good Samaritan. In that parable, an unlikely hero, a Samaritan, stops to help a Jewish man in need. Jesus points to his compassionate actions as an example of what it looks like to love your neighbor—an essential part of what God requires of us. What Jesus teaches Martha counterbalances the lesson of that parable.

Martha has invited Jesus into her and her sister's home, and this, of course, includes preparing a meal. I want you to place yourself in this scene. Martha has just invited Jesus and his twelve disciples into the home, where she will now feed them. My family recently had thirteen people over for dinner. We had burgers and hot dogs, chips and beans and coleslaw, watermelon, and brownies. Even that simple dinner required a trip to the grocery store and an hour of preparation. LaVon prepared parts of the meal, got everyone drinks, and set the table. I cooked on the grill. I can say that if LaVon had left me to do everything and she stood around visiting with our guests, I'd have been very, very frustrated, and vice versa.

But that is precisely what is happening here. Martha is in the kitchen frantically preparing a meal for Jesus, his disciples, and any others who may have followed him in. This is no small task. Many see Martha as the diligent, responsible older sister. She is the doer. Meanwhile, the younger sister, Mary, seems oblivious to the pots clanging in the kitchen as she sits at the feet of Jesus, soaking in every word. Martha grows more and more resentful with each passing minute until she finally comes to Jesus saying, "Lord, don't you care that this lousy sister of mine has left me to prepare this entire meal for all of you by myself? Tell her to come help!"

It was assumed in this time that women's place was in the kitchen. It was men who sat with the wise teachers. The saying "sit at someone's feet" was already in use at this time to describe learning from another. It is what disciples do with their teachers, to sit at their feet and learn from them. As we noted, first-century rabbis did not invite women to be disciples. The Jewish Mishnah goes so far as to say, "Let thy house be a meeting-house for the Sages and sit amid the dust of their feet and drink in their words with thirst... [but] talk not much with womankind."[8]

Understanding this context helps us see the difference between Mary's behavior and Martha's. Here is Mary sitting among the men, acting like an equal with the male disciples, taking in the words of Jesus. Mary is violating the gender roles and social customs of the day in order to listen to Jesus. Martha was fulfilling the gender role of her time, acting like a woman was supposed to act in the first century. But she was missing out on the words of life Jesus was offering. What does Jesus say? "Martha, Martha, you are worried and distracted by many things. One thing is necessary. Mary has chosen the better part. It won't be taken away from her." In essence, Jesus was saying, "Martha, stop feeling trapped by the role others put you in. I'm here now, in your home. You're missing what matters most."

David Garland in his commentary on Luke notes, "Ironically, Martha addresses Jesus as 'Lord,' but it is Mary 'who sits at Jesus' feet and listens to his word.'"[9] This story points, once again, to Jesus's desire to lift up those who have been pushed back into the kitchen by society.

> ## We are to selflessly serve others, even the stranger—this is what it means to love your neighbor. But we must also make time to listen, to learn, to fellowship with Jesus.

To Martha's credit, she is not just doing what the societal role is; she is genuinely seeking to serve and to bless her guests, particularly Jesus. She is doing what Jesus teaches in the parable of the good Samaritan that Luke places *right before* this story of Martha and Mary. It is as if Luke is intending for these two stories to counterbalance each other. We are to selflessly serve others, even the stranger—this is what it means to love your neighbor. But we must also make time to listen, to learn, to fellowship with Jesus, which is what Mary is teaching us.

There are Christians I know who live out their faith primarily by doing. They are teaching children's Sunday school but never make it to worship. They are serving in the soup kitchen but seldom spend time in prayer or scripture study. And there are those who pray for hours a week, and attend worship every weekend, but who do little to serve those who are in need. The good Samaritan and the story of Mary and Martha go hand-in-hand to lead us to a balanced faith of fellowship with Christ and serving others.

In this story, Martha is being the good Samaritan as Mary sits at Jesus's feet. And Jesus affirms Mary over Martha. There is a time for us to listen, to simply be with Jesus, to imbibe his word and spirit. Many of us are doers, fewer of us are contemplative. This story and the parable of the good Samaritan are both important. In other books, I've taught about the concept of *ora et labora*, a Latin phrase that means "pray and work." We spend time in prayer, in scripture study, in contemplation, in worship, *and* we serve others. We need to be both Mary and Martha. But don't miss the bigger picture here—Jesus is breaking down the societal barriers inviting women to join the male disciples as they sit at his feet.

Saints and Sinners at a Meal with Jesus

The story of Mary and Martha occurs at a meal. So do many of the other great stories in Luke. In fact, meals are a major setting for Jesus's ministry in Luke. There are at least ten stories in Luke that happen around a meal, and seven are unique to Luke's Gospel.

At times, Jesus was criticized for eating and drinking with sinners. They said of him, "Look, a glutton and a drunkard, a friend of tax collectors and sinners." But I love this about Jesus. I'm reminded that the word *companion* comes from the Latin, *com panis—com* means with and *panis* means bread. A companion is one you break bread with. Jesus is accused of being a companion with the sinners—with outsiders and outcasts and outlaws.

But I want to draw your attention to a particular meal where Jesus was eating at the home of those who saw themselves as pious.

He was eating at the home of a religious leader, a Pharisee named Simon.

The Pharisees were a sect of about six thousand people in Jesus's day who studied and taught the law of Moses. They were often rabbis of local synagogues, though some were itinerant preachers. They were highly respected for their piety, for their grasp of the law, and for encouraging ordinary people to live holy lives. The name *Pharisee* is thought by some to come from the Hebrew word *parushi* which means "separated"—perhaps a reference to their efforts at being separated from sin and sinners.

Some Pharisees were drawn to Jesus, or at least were very curious about him. In some ways he shared much in common with them. Three times in Luke's Gospel, Pharisees invite Jesus over for dinner. After his death and resurrection, a number of Pharisees became his followers, including the apostle Paul.

But the Pharisees were most often frustrated by Jesus. He defined piety differently than they did and interpreted the law in ways they did not. He nearly always put people before rules. While they separated themselves from sinners, Jesus befriended them.

Simon, a Pharisee, invited Jesus to his home for a meal; but there were small slights, little insults that were intended to make clear that Simon thought himself above Jesus. Simon did not provide the customary welcome for a respected guest, a kiss on the cheek. He did not provide a basin of water for Jesus to wash his feet as he entered the home. And there was no scented oil that would be applied to freshen up after a long day. The neglect of this common hospitality was a subtle way for Simon to put Jesus in his place.

Jesus didn't say anything, he just sat down at the table and joined in the conversation as the meal began. Just then an uninvited guest, a woman, forced her way into Simon's home, perhaps a courtyard that served as his banquet hall. As we learned in the last story, having a woman entering the banquet hall who was not a servant was unusual enough, but Luke describes her as "a woman from the city, a sinner." All people were sinners, but here she is known for her sinful life. Simon knows "what kind of woman she is." Was she an alcoholic, an addict, an adulteress, a thief, or, as many suppose, a prostitute?

The reader is left to suppose why she had come looking for Jesus. She must have had a previous encounter with Jesus. I imagine her hearing him speaking to a crowd earlier in the day. I picture his gaze meeting hers in that crowd. He could see the guilt and shame she carried with her. And I imagine him telling a story, perhaps the story of the prodigal son, that proclaimed God's mercy and love for sinful people.

Whatever her sin, and whatever happened earlier in the day that the reader is not privy to, she's heard Jesus is eating at the home of the Pharisee and she's determined to see him. Imagine how much courage and determination it must have taken for this sinful woman to barge into the home of a Pharisee of all people. Her eyes quickly scan the room for the man she saw earlier in the day. She has in her hand a small alabaster jar containing what was likely her most prized possession: a fragrant oil of great value. A similar story, perhaps the same story with different details, occurs in Mark 14. There the oil was said to be worth a year's wages.

Luke tells us, "Standing behind him at his feet and crying, she began to wet his feet with her tears. She wiped them with her hair, kissed them, and poured the oil on them" (Luke 7:38). Simon the Pharisee is shocked by what he sees, and Luke tells us what he is thinking. "If this man were a prophet, he would know what kind of woman is touching him. He would know that she is a sinner" (Luke 7:39).

I want to pause here and ask if you've ever been a Pharisee in this sense of the word—judgmental in your thoughts, thinking things you'd never say aloud? What do you see when you look at others? Do you see their sins, or their humanity and their heart? Do you find yourself judging them or having compassion on them? Do you look down on them for the clothes they wear, the words they speak, the sins they've committed, the life or lifestyle they lead? Or do you see them as dearly loved children of God? I have been Simon the Pharisee. I've often told my congregation that I am a recovering Pharisee who sometimes "falls off the wagon."

Jesus speaks, telling Simon a parable. "A certain lender had two debtors. One owed enough money to pay five hundred people for a day's work. The other owed enough money for fifty. When they couldn't pay, the lender forgave the debts of them both. Which of them will love him more?" Simon replied, "I suppose the one who had the largest debt canceled." Jesus said, "You have judged correctly" (Luke 7:41-43).

It is what Jesus says next that really gets me. He says, "Simon, do you see this woman?" He points out that she did for him what Simon refused to do as the host—she kissed his feet, she washed them and poured oil over them—all the simple acts of hospitality Simon, in his pridefulness, refused to do. But it is the question, "Do you see this woman?" that moves me. Simon saw a sinner. Jesus saw a woman in pain, broken, ashamed. Jesus saw someone who needed grace, not judgment. Jesus saw a dearly loved daughter of God.

I titled this section "saints and sinners at a meal with Jesus." By the story's end I have to ask, who was the saint, and who was the sinner?

Jesus Sees You

This is one of the stories that, when I read it as a fourteen-year-old, led me to love Jesus. This is a picture of the character and love of Christ, of the gift of his mercy, his willingness to forgive us and heal us and make us new. He is the Lord of the second chance. How grateful I am for that.

And that question he asked Simon, "Do you see this woman?" Clearly Simon had not seen her. But Jesus did see her. He saw not what she had done, but who she was to God, and who she could be.

Jesus sees *you*. He sees your pain, your brokenness, your hurts and heartaches and hang-ups. And he sees who you were meant to be. He sees you as a dearly loved child of God.

Jesus sees *you*. He sees your pain, your brokenness, your hurts and heartaches and hang-ups. And he sees who you were meant to be. He sees you as a dearly loved child of God. And he says to you, as he did to her, Your sins are forgiven, your faith has saved you, go in peace.

Jesus's Concern for Women

Which takes me back to my granddaughter, Stella. I know that Jesus sees her, knows her, and loves her. She is not an object to be desired or scorned by men, but a human being with dignity and sacred worth. What I hope is that society, men in particular, will see her and others the way Jesus saw the women he interacted and ministered with.

And when she grows up, will she join the 743 million women who have been victims of domestic violence? Or the 81 percent of women who reported being sexually harassed (including 17.5 percent who have experienced sexual harassment *in the church*)?[10] Will she still earn 84 percent of what a man earns for the same job? Will there be more opportunities for her in the church, the workplace, government? Or will 91 percent of top corporate jobs still belong to men?

Will she grow up in a world where women are seen, not as objects to be pursued, but as people to be valued, who can pursue their dreams, and where there is an equality of opportunity? A world where men will see her as a human being?

Jesus shows us the way in Luke's Gospel. Let's follow him.

3

PARABLES FROM THE UNDERSIDE

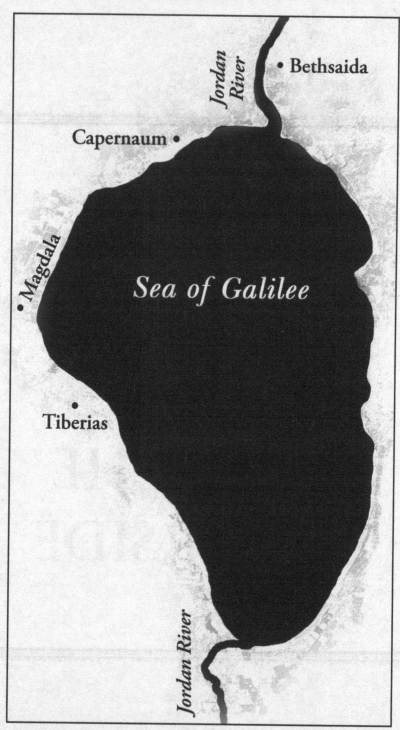

Much of the ministry and teaching of Jesus occurred around the Sea of Galilee before he "determined to go to Jerusalem" (Luke 9:51).

3

PARABLES FROM THE UNDERSIDE

Jesus told this parable to certain people who had convinced themselves that they were righteous and who looked on everyone else with disgust: "Two people went up to the temple to pray. One was a Pharisee and the other a tax collector. The Pharisee stood and prayed about himself with these words, 'God, I thank you that I'm not like everyone else— crooks, evildoers, adulterers—or even like this tax collector. I fast twice a week. I give a tenth of everything I receive.' But the tax collector stood at a distance. He wouldn't even lift his eyes to look toward heaven. Rather, he struck his chest and said, 'God, show mercy to me, a sinner.' I tell you, this person went down to his home justified rather than the Pharisee. All who lift themselves up will be brought low, and those who make themselves low will be lifted up."

(Luke 18:9-14)

I've always been more rock and roll than country. I grew up on the Beatles and the Rolling Stones. But in the last few years I've found myself spending more time listening to country and western music. The songs I love are those that tell a story that gets me thinking about the meaning of life. In the introduction I mentioned Garth Brooks's "Friends in Low Places." I loved Glen Campbell's final album, "Adios," recorded after he had announced he had Alzheimer's. His longtime friend Carl Jackson had to stand next to him as he sang, feeding him the lyrics one line at a time because he couldn't remember them.

39

It would be his farewell album, and the story of how he recorded it so touched me that I listened to the album hundreds of times by the time of his death in 2017. Recently I was driving with my granddaughter listening to Jordan Davis and Luke Bryan singing about the advice of an eighty-year-old man about making life count in their hit song "Buy Dirt." I began crying as I tried to explain to Stella why this song spoke to me.

Jesus was a storyteller. His stories were called parables, and they were intended to teach his hearers about the meaning of life and faith, who God is and what he longs for from us. And, as we're about to see, so many of Jesus's parables spoke to and about outsiders, outcasts, and outlaws.

There are forty-nine different parables recorded in Matthew, Mark, and Luke. Nine appear in all three Gospels. Two appear only in Mark. Eight appear only in Matthew. And sixteen appear only in Luke. That's a lot of unique parables that Luke records on the lips of Jesus. I'm going to draw your attention to three of these sixteen found only in Luke, and through them we'll see two more dimensions to Jesus's passion for lifting up the lowly. But first a word about parables.

Speaking in Parables

The parables Jesus told were sometimes simple analogies or similes where he likens the kingdom of God to, for instance, a mustard seed (Luke 13:18-19). But often they were more detailed stories that ordinary people could relate to—fictional stories illustrating some spiritual truth about God or faith or how we're meant to live. These stories were easy to remember, they came from everyday life, and they contained one or occasionally two or three spiritual truths. They often contrasted the life and heart that God intended with the life and heart of those who fail to "get it"—who fail to do God's will.

Some were easy to understand. But a few left his hearers, and still leave contemporary readers, scratching their heads. An example of the perplexing parables is the parable of the dishonest manager in Luke 16:1-9, of which there are no less than four interpretations, none of which makes perfect sense, at least not to me. Perhaps this is why the parables were sometimes called riddles.

As you read the parables, you'll notice that often Jesus has two or more contrasting characters or objects—two sons, four types of soil a seed falls upon, a spiritually proud person and one who is humble, a rich but indifferent man and a poor man who suffers at his gate. As you study the parables, always look to the context: What has just happened before the parable? What has Jesus just said? What have others just said? Who is Jesus speaking to? Once you are clear about the context—and Luke is great at giving the context so we don't miss the point—we can ask two questions:

1. In what ways am I like each of the characters or objects in the parable?
2. What does Jesus want me to know, think, or do in response to this parable?

As we consider three of the most loved parables of Jesus, found only in Luke's Gospel, what I want you to notice is how each demonstrates Jesus's concern for humbling the proud while lifting up the lowly.

The Parable of the Pharisee and the Tax Collector

Let's begin with the parable of the Pharisee and the tax collector, found in Luke 18:9-14. Verse 9 tells us the context for this parable: "Jesus told this parable to certain people who had convinced themselves that they were righteous and who looked on everyone else with disgust." Can you picture these "righteous" folks? We saw an example in the last chapter in Simon the Pharisee and his judgment of the sinful woman. Remember what we read about how the first-century Pharisees looked down on the 'Am ha-Arez.

An increasing number of people in the United States claim no religion. This growing group is sometimes referred to as the "nones" (those who have had no church or faith) and the "dones" (those who have left church after feeling turned off). Ask the nones why they have never considered church, or the dones why they left, and you are likely to find somewhere in their responses a frustration or hurt related to the judgmentalism, hypercriticism, and religious hypocrisy they have experienced from church folks. When I've probed about hypocrisy, I've found the problem isn't that religious people sin. Everyone sins, and the nones and dones understand that. The problem is that religious people are blind to their own sin but are far too willing to communicate their judgment of the sins of others. This was the sense you get from Jesus's criticism of some of the Pharisees.

So, let's take a look at what Jesus says in the parable of the Pharisee and the tax collector.

"Two people went up to the temple to pray. One was a Pharisee and the other a tax collector. The Pharisee stood and prayed about himself with these words, 'God, I thank you that I'm not like everyone else—crooks, evildoers, adulterers—or even like this tax collector. I fast twice a week. I give a tenth of everything I receive.' But the tax collector stood at a distance. He wouldn't even lift his eyes to look toward heaven. Rather, he struck his chest and said, 'God, show mercy to me, a sinner.' I tell you, this person went down to his home justified rather than the Pharisee. All who lift themselves up will be brought low, and those who make themselves low will be lifted up."

(Luke 18:10-14)

Let's consider our questions:

1. In what ways am I like each of the characters or objects in the parable?
2. What does Jesus want me to know, think, or do in response to this parable?

We've already noted the context, found in verse 9, "Jesus told this parable to certain people who had convinced themselves that they were righteous and who looked on everyone else with disgust." Regarding the first question, in what ways have you ever been like the Pharisee who, seeing the tax collector, felt superior and self-righteous, and who acted with judgmentalism rather than compassion? I have been the Pharisee in this parable at times and I suspect you have as well. Have you ever been the tax collector, so keenly aware of your guilt and shame that you could only beat your breast and pray, "God, show mercy to me, a sinner"?

Am I the judgmental, spiritually prideful person who can't see his own sin? Or am I the person who realizes that I'm as much of a sinner as anyone else, grieves my sin, and cries out for God's grace?

I read this parable and ask, Jesus, am I the Pharisee or the tax collector? Am I the judgmental, spiritually prideful person who can't see his own sin? Or am I the person who realizes that I'm as much of a sinner as anyone else, grieves my sin, and cries out for God's grace?

As I noted in chapter 2, I'm a recovering Pharisee who sometimes falls off the wagon. My hunch is, so are you. It is so easy to judge others, to assume the worst of them and, in the process, to feel a spiritual pride, thanking God that we're "not like that sinner over there."

Of the seven deadly sins, the church recognizes that pride is the deadliest of all and is at the heart of nearly all the others.

Let's consider our second question: what does Jesus want us to know, or think, or do in response to this parable? Jesus tells us at the end of the parable what our response should be. "All who lift themselves up will be brought low, and those who make themselves low will be lifted up." Notice this is the same thing Mary said in the Magnificat. It strikes at the heart of Luke's main theme. We are to, in the words of James 4:10, "Humble [ourselves] before the Lord, and he will lift [us] up." This idea is found throughout scripture. Jesus will make this point again at the Last Supper when his disciples are secretly debating which of them is the greatest, and he interrupts them and says, "The greatest among you must become like a person of lower status and the leader like a servant" (Luke 22:26).

The number of practicing Christians in America has been in decline for over a decade, and the decline has been steep, a drop of between 30 and 50 percent according to the 2020 State of the Church report issued by Barna.[1] Many have sought to understand what's behind this dramatic decline. Among the answers, as already noted, is the very thing the Pharisee in this parable was illustrating: hypocrisy, self-righteousness, and judgmentalism that both Christians and non-Christians have experienced in churches. The Pharisee in us is killing the church by driving others away from the Christ we proclaim.

God, please help us to be less like the "righteous" Pharisee, and more like the humble tax collector. Please help us to humble ourselves before you.

The Parable of the Prodigal Son

While Christians have found a way to drive people away from Christ, Jesus was constantly surrounded by those the religious folks called "sinners and tax collectors." We see that as the context for our next parable in Luke 15:1: "All the tax collectors and sinners were gathering around Jesus to listen to him." He was irresistible to them. His kindness, his depth, his love and mercy, his lack of judgment (Jesus seemed to reserve his judgment for the self-righteous religious leaders), his willingness to stop and meet their needs, and his ability to speak about God in ways they understood were all compelling. People felt God's presence when they were with him.

Now look at the next verse, Luke 15:2: "The Pharisees and legal experts were grumbling, saying, 'This man welcomes sinners and eats with them.'" These opening verses of Luke 15, the fact of crowds of tax collectors and sinners being drawn to Jesus, and the religious folks' irritation with Jesus's embrace of these people, his willingness to befriend them by breaking bread with them, serve as the reason Jesus tells the next three parables in Luke: the parables of the lost sheep, the lost coin, and the lost son (the prodigal son).

You'll read all three of these parables if you follow the reading plan that accompanies this book (found at AdamHamilton.com/Luke.) Here we'll focus on the most famous of these parables, the parable of the lost son/the prodigal son. I picture the large crowd of sinners and tax collectors surrounding Jesus as he tells this parable. Just beyond them, I see the scribes and Pharisees, listening and looking down upon the crowd (physically and metaphorically), as Jesus spoke to this "riffraff" of unobservant Jews saying:

"A certain man had two sons. The younger son said to his father, 'Father, give me my share of the inheritance.' Then the father divided his estate between them. Soon afterward, the younger son gathered everything together and took a trip to a land far away. There, he wasted his wealth through extravagant living."

(Luke 15:11-13)

The younger of two sons demands his share of the inheritance from his father while his father is still alive. The nerve of the young man. Such a request dishonors his father, for the inheritance was meant first to sustain a parent until death, and only then passed on.

And the father, surprisingly, gives the boy his share. The son leaves with his money, goes to a far-off country, and wastes his father's hard-earned money on wild living. The word *prodigal* means wasteful, reckless, or squandering in the use of wealth. No wonder this boy is called the prodigal son.

The Pharisees and legal experts look over this crowd and know that Jesus is speaking about these sinners and tax collectors. They wonder if Jesus will call out this crowd for their sinful and prodigal ways. But Jesus continues:

> *"When [the younger son] had used up his resources, a severe food shortage arose in that country and he began to be in need. He hired himself out to one of the citizens of that country, who sent him into his fields to feed pigs. He longed to eat his fill from what the pigs ate, but no one gave him anything."*

> *(Luke 15:14-16)*

The sinners and the saints in this crowd all would have recognized how dire this young man's situation was. Pigs were unclean animals, and if you were a Jew, working on the pig farm was nearly as low as you could go. But wishing to eat what the pigs ate? That was really "hitting bottom." I've known people like this, who were so lost that they lost their minds or hearts or souls. They sold their bodies, committed crimes, gave up their jobs or family. Often they were addicted. Sometimes they simply wandered, like a sheep, little by little, away from the fold of God.

Notice what Jesus said happened next:

> *"When he came to his senses, he said, 'How many of my father's hired hands have more than enough food, but I'm starving to death! I will get up and go to my father, and say to him, "Father, I have sinned against heaven and against you. I no longer deserve to be called your son. Take me on as one of your hired hands."' So he got up and went to his father."*

> *(Luke 15:17-20)*

The young man determines to return to his father and repent, apologizing and seeking to be restored to his father's estate. He no longer hopes he could be accepted back as a son, though perhaps as a household servant. The Pharisees know how the father will respond to this son; surely he will *punish him harshly* for his profligate life and the way he dishonored his father. But look at what Jesus actually says about the father's response:

> "While he was still a long way off, **his father saw him** and was **moved with compassion. His father ran to him, hugged him, and kissed him**. Then his son said, 'Father, I have sinned against heaven and against you. I no longer deserve to be called your son.' But the father said to his servants, 'Quickly, bring out the best robe and put it on him! Put a ring on his finger and sandals on his feet! Fetch the fattened calf and slaughter it. We must celebrate with feasting because this son of mine was dead and has come back to life! He was lost and is found!' And they **began to celebrate**."
>
> (Luke 15:20-24, emphasis added)

I picture Jesus turning to the crowd of sinners, with the Pharisees listening in, and saying, "*This* is what God is like!" Imagine that kind of love and mercy! Even before the boy asked for mercy the father ran to him, hugged him, and kissed him. What a different picture of God Jesus painted for the tax collectors and sinners than the picture of God they learned from their treatment by the Pharisees.

Jesus teaches that God is God of the second chance. God loves us relentlessly and refuses to give up on us. God takes us back despite our foolish, prodigal ways.

Tax collectors were, as you likely know, despised by most Jews because they had seemingly sold their souls to the Romans, purchasing the right to collect Rome's taxes and making their money on the additional portion they collected from their fellow Jews. They were outsiders, outcasts, *and* considered outlaws or thieves. Yet Jesus is regularly associated with them, breaking bread with them, befriending them, and offering them grace. Once again, Jesus *sees* them. He knows they are alienated from their people and unwelcome in the synagogue. Can you imagine how shocking and scandalous it was when Jesus called Levi, a tax collector, to be his disciple? Or, when he chose to eat in the home of Zacchaeus, the *chief* tax collector of Jericho?

Jesus was also a friend of sinners. The Greek word for sinners here is *hamartolous* from the Greek word *hamartia*, which is usually translated as "sin" but literally means to miss the mark. Often used in archery to describe an arrow that veered off course, it was a fitting word to describe the lives of these multitudes who had, like us, veered off God's path again and again. They had turned aside from God's will. And what did you do with sinners? If you were a Pharisee, you separated yourself from them. But if you were Jesus, you sought them out, befriended them and offered them grace, and worked to bring them back to God. *This* is what led me to love Jesus and to long to follow him.

The parable announced grace to the prodigals of that day and today. But this is not the end of the parable. Look again at Luke 15. The older brother returns home and hears the celebration his father has put together for his good-for-nothing little brother. And hearing the music, he becomes furious. He refuses to come into the home. His father comes out and begs him to come in. The older brother responded:

> "Look, I've served you all these years, and I never disobeyed your instruction. Yet you've never given me as much as a young goat so I could celebrate with my friends. But when this son of yours returned, after gobbling up your estate on prostitutes, you slaughtered the fattened calf for him."
>
> (Luke 15:29-30)

Suddenly the Pharisees in the crowd are nodding their heads, for they identify with this older brother. Notice that Jesus doesn't condemn them for their feelings. I suspect you and I might have had the same feelings if we were the older brother in this story. It's easy to be resentful of the younger brother, to feel like this grace the father has shown is unfair. Grace *is* unfair. None of us deserve it. That's what makes it grace.

The parable ends with Jesus reporting the words of the father to the older brother, presumably the words of *The Father* to the Pharisees: "Then his father said, 'Son, you are always with me, and everything I have is yours. But we had to celebrate and be glad because this brother of yours was dead and is alive. He was lost and is found'" (Luke 15:31-32).

In so many of the Gospel stories in Luke, we're invited to consider who were really the sinners and the saints.

Again, I love that Jesus was trying, in one parable, to speak to both the younger and older brothers, to the sinners and the saints. And, as in so many of the Gospel stories in Luke, we're invited to consider who were really the sinners and the saints in this parable. He wanted *both* to know that they were loved by the Father in this parable.

Recently, I preached on the parable of the prodigal son and asked folks on Facebook if any of them had been the prodigal son. I had a couple of dozen people who sent me direct messages to tell me their stories. One woman wrote,

> I was an addict in active addiction for over ten years, I cursed God, stayed away from my family for years, and basically hid myself from anything that mattered. One day I asked God for help, and my life has drastically changed. I was baptized by a Resurrection pastor, have been clean

49

and sober over two years now. I have my daughter, family, a fiancé, and 2 jobs, but most importantly, I have Jesus, with whom I have an intimate relationship.

Another described growing up in a United Methodist church, very involved and committed. She went away to college, got involved in a college campus ministry, and one night, when one of the leaders in the group asked her over for a date, he sexually assaulted her. She wrote,

> After that night, I turned away from the church. I headed down a path of self-destruction. I would drink until I blacked out. I became bulimic. I was suicidal. I had no respect for my body...I guess you might say it wasn't "mine" anymore. I tried therapy and quit. I tried anti-depressants, and quit those too. I felt like I was nothing and deserved to be in that dark place.

She believed that somehow the assault was her fault, that she had sinned. She went on to describe how, years later, she met the man who became her husband. She wrote,

> I gave therapy and anti-depressants another try. I started going back to church...accepting that sometimes bad things happen to good people, that I wasn't "damaged goods," and that God still loved me.
>
> I had been so angry with God...and I felt so ashamed and unworthy of His love and grace. Looking back, I see the ways in which He was walking with me. Giving me strength. Putting people in my path to help me along the way. I am grateful for His love. I'm also so grateful for Resurrection; this church welcomed us with open arms. It has changed our lives.

I don't know your story. You may be the older son who has never fallen away and always been faithful to God. Because of that, it may be harder to have compassion for the prodigals. The parable is meant to remind you that God never gives up on those who turn away, and if we really love God, we're meant to be a part of welcoming and celebrating when those people come home.

But if you are someone who has made a mess of your life, running away from God, doing what you thought would make you happy only to find it left you feeling lost and alone, God has never given up on you, and he longs for you to come home.

The Parable of the Rich Man and Lazarus

Let's turn to the third parable, the parable of the rich man and Lazarus (Luke 16:19-31). To see the context for this parable, we need to look at Luke 16:14: "The Pharisees, who were money-lovers, heard all this and sneered at Jesus." In the verses leading up to this in Luke 16, Jesus had been speaking about wealth, maintaining a right relationship to it, the importance of giving it away, and how we cannot serve both God and money. The Pharisees sneered at something Jesus said about money. Luke then tells us something we have not heard up to this point: the Pharisees were "money-lovers."

Throughout Luke, the Pharisees are a foil for Jesus. They represent a form of religion that misses the point. And there is no doubt that there were Pharisees like the ones we read about in the parables and see in the stories throughout Luke. Some scholars believe the Gospel of Luke was written at a time when the Pharisees and other religious authorities were excommunicating Jewish Christians from the synagogues in the decades following the destruction of Jerusalem, and that Luke's descriptions of the Pharisees reflect the growing animosity between the Christian community and the Pharisees.

But it is important to note that this caricature of the Pharisees does not tell the whole story. Theologically, Jesus shared much in common with the Pharisees; the Pharisees were drawn to Jesus for this reason. In Luke 5:17 we read, "One day when he was teaching, Pharisees and legal experts were sitting nearby. They had come from every village in Galilee and Judea, and from Jerusalem." They were sitting nearby watching and listening to him. Three times in Luke's Gospel, Pharisees invite Jesus to their home for dinner. In John we find Nicodemus, a Pharisee, who comes to Jesus as a secret follower and later helps with Jesus's burial. In Acts, volume 2 of Luke's work, there are many Pharisees who became followers of Jesus, including the apostle Paul. In Acts 5:17-39 a well-known Pharisee named Gamaliel speaks up and calls for restraint toward the apostles. Likewise, in Acts 23:9, Pharisees speak up for Paul.

My point is that while the word *Pharisee* is today synonymous with self-righteousness, judgmentalism, legalism, and religious people who miss the point, in the first century, there were many Pharisees who were good and pious and drawn to Jesus. And yes, there were also many who were jealous of Jesus, infuriated by his interpretation of scripture, his violation of their rules, and his willingness to associate with the *'Am ha-Arez*.

Let's return to the parable of the rich man and Lazarus that Luke tells us was in response to the money-loving Pharisees:

> *"There was a certain rich man who clothed himself in purple and fine linen, and who feasted luxuriously every day. At his gate lay a certain poor man named Lazarus who was covered with sores. Lazarus longed to eat the crumbs that fell from the rich man's table. Instead, dogs would come and lick his sores."*
>
> *(Luke 16:19-21)*

Once again, we see Jesus contrasting one person with another, not an older and younger brother in this parable, but a rich man and a poor man. Jesus doesn't name the rich man, though he is often called "Dives" from the Latin word for rich. Jesus *does tell us* the name of the poor man. His name is Lazarus, which means "God has helped." This is the only time in all the parables that Jesus names a character, which means that name had some significance to Jesus.[2] This story will teach us about God's concern for the poor and God's punishment for the wealthy who fail to see the poor, and who lack compassion and do not stop to help.

Like many of Jesus's parables, it does what humorist Finley Peter Dunne said the job of a journalist was: to "comfort the afflicted and afflict the comfortable."[3] We see that in the next line of the parable:

> *"The poor man died and was carried by angels to Abraham's side. The rich man also died and was buried. While being tormented in the place of the dead, he looked up and saw Abraham at a distance with Lazarus at his side."*

> *(Luke 16:22-23)*

The main point of this parable is unmistakable: If you ignore the poor, step over them, do nothing to help them, you've utterly failed at what it means to be a human, a Jew, or a follower of Jesus. The consequences of such a failure are serious.

And it promises that, as Jesus says in Luke's version of the Beatitudes, "Happy are you who hunger now, because you will be satisfied" (Luke 6:21). This beatitude, and this parable, once more illustrate the "great reversal" in Luke's Gospel. Lazarus is in the bosom of Abraham, and Dives burning in Gehenna, in the place of suffering in the realm of the dead.

What do you think the rich man would say, or what thoughts came to his heart each day as he justified to himself ignoring Lazarus at his gate? I can imagine the thoughts: "Unemployment is so low, he could surely get a job if he wanted to work. Why should I take my hard-earned money and help this man? If I do, he'll just want more tomorrow. God helps those who help themselves. If I help, he's probably just going to take the money and buy alcohol. Where are his family? They should be helping him. He's obviously sick. He might be contagious." I'm sure there are plenty more thoughts that could have wandered across Dives's mind when he stepped over Lazarus.

The consequences of the rich man's disregard for Lazarus in life have eternal significance. God brings aid and comfort to those who suffer in life, while those who step over and ignore the poor and suffering will themselves suffer. Once again we see in this parable the same message we first heard in Mary's Magnificat in Luke 1:

> *He has scattered those with arrogant thoughts and proud*
> *inclinations.*
> *He has pulled the powerful down from their thrones*
> *and lifted up the lowly.*
> *He has filled the hungry with good things*
> *and sent the rich away empty-handed.*
>
> (Luke 1:51b-53)

The parable of the rich man and Lazarus is not alone in Luke in pointing to Christ's teaching on caring for the lowly, the poor, and the sick or injured. Among the most famous parables Jesus tells is the parable of the good Samaritan, which, like the parable of the rich man and Lazarus, is found only in Luke's Gospel.

Among the most famous parables Jesus tells is the parable of the good Samaritan, which, like the parable of the rich man and Lazarus, is found only in Luke's Gospel.

In Luke 10 a legal expert asks Jesus, "What must I do to inherit eternal life?" Jesus replies with a question, "What is written in the Law? How do you interpret it?" The man responds, "You must love the Lord your God with all your heart, with all your being, with all your strength, and with all your mind, and love your neighbor as yourself." Jesus said, "Do this and you will live." But the man asks a follow-up question, "Who is my neighbor?" (10:25-29). Which is another way of asking, "Which people don't I have to love?"

Jesus responds with the parable of the good Samaritan. We'll touch on this parable a bit more in the next chapter, but for now, simply notice in the good Samaritan that our neighbor is anyone who needs us. In the parable, a man is accosted by robbers, beaten, and left for dead. Two religious people walk by and pass to the other side of the road (just as Dives seems routinely to have done regarding Lazarus).

Once more, we're left to imagine what the priest and Levite were thinking as they ignored the plight of the injured man. But along comes a Samaritan, of a race and religion that most Jews considered unclean. The Samaritans were, literally, the original *'Am ha-Arez*. But it is the Samaritan, of all people, who stops to help the injured man, bandaging his wounds, placing him on his donkey, and providing a place for him to recuperate, along with food, clothing, and medical care. This is what it means to love your neighbor. This is what it means to be human. And this is what Jesus expects of his followers.

These two parables, the rich man and Lazarus and the good Samaritan, are just two examples of Jesus's emphasis on lifting up the poor in Luke. We see it in Jesus's very first sermon in Luke 4:18, where he quotes from Isaiah, "The Spirit of the Lord is upon me, because he has anointed me to preach good news *to the poor*" (emphasis added). We see it when we contrast Matthew's recounting of the Beatitudes with Luke's. Matthew seems to spiritualize Jesus's words about poverty and hunger, but in Luke the blessed are really poor and hungry. Matthew has, "Blessed are the poor *in spirit*..." where Luke records Jesus saying, "Blessed are the poor..." In Matthew, Jesus says, "Blessed are those who hunger and thirst *after righteousness*..." But in Luke, Jesus says, "Blessed are you who are hungry now...." And Luke includes these warnings with the Beatitudes that Matthew does not: "How terrible for you who are rich, because you have already received your comfort. How terrible for you who have plenty now, because you will be hungry" (Luke 6:24-25).

This is another example of the "great reversal" in Luke's Gospel, in which the wealthy and powerful are brought down, but the poor and powerless are lifted up.

Jesus speaks a lot about riches in Luke, because even first-century peasants struggled in their relationship with money. Among the most powerful statements Jesus makes on this is in Luke 12:15, where two brothers were arguing about their inheritance and Jesus says, "Watch out! Guard yourself against all kinds of greed. After all, one's life isn't determined by one's possessions, even when someone is very wealthy." There, in Luke 12:16-20, he goes on to tell another parable about a foolish man who keeps building bigger barns to hold all of his possessions. Later in that same chapter Jesus speaks to what God expects of those who have plenty, like the rich man with Lazarus: "Much will be demanded from everyone who has been given much, and from the one who has been entrusted with much, even more will be asked" (Luke 12:48). Dives failed to understand this fundamental law of life, that the blessings we receive come with a responsibility.

I'm guessing your church routinely seeks to embody the good Samaritan's heart and spirit. One of our membership requirements at Resurrection is that our members give to and serve the poor or organizations that serve them. We do this together as a church in significant ways, but we also invite people to do this on their own—to be more like the Samaritan who saw the man who was in need, rather than Dives (or the priest and Levite) who walked by pretending not to see.

I have the joy of seeing examples of this all the time. Recently it was two elementary school children whose birthdays were near the same date. For their party, they asked their friends to bring food to be donated to an area food pantry in lieu of gifts. I see this all the time, kids making a choice to be the Samaritan instead of Dives.

Do you remember what the name Lazarus means? *God has helped.* How does God help? He uses people like you and me as instruments of blessing. There are so many ways to do this. I think of the skin lesions Lazarus suffered with and how one of our members, a pharmacist, just opened a pharmacy for low-income people. Or my friend Gary who, as I write these words, is in Ukraine delivering medical supplies. Or our Food Mobile, run by volunteers who drive our mobile grocery store to "food deserts" in Kansas City where there is not ready and close access to fresh fruits and vegetables, meats, and dairy products. These are all volunteers seeking to be more like the Samaritan than Dives.

As I was finishing this chapter, I was listening to Malcolm Gladwell's podcast, *Revisionist History.* The episode I was listening to was titled, "I Was a Stranger and You Welcomed Me," drawn from the words of a parable of Jesus in Matthew, the parable of the sheep and the goats, another parable pointing to Jesus's concern that his disciples help others. Gladwell was talking with a group of older adults, friends of his parents, in the town where he grew up. They were talking about the events of 1979. That year hundreds of thousands of people fled Vietnam by boat. Most were Vietnamese of Chinese descent, known as the Hoa. The Vietnamese government was, at the time, a repressive regime. They confiscated property of those who had fought alongside Americans in the war. They forced people from their homes and into labor camps. Many people tried to flee the country. Somewhere between two hundred thousand to four hundred thousand perished at sea trying to escape their home country.

Churches in the US and Canada began asking their governments to increase their quotas of immigrants. But there were many who resisted these ideas. Those who resisted had well-articulated reasons for not accepting more of the refugees: the Hoa might be a threat to American and Canadian jobs, or to our security. How could we know they were not Chinese or Vietnamese spies? How could we afford the costs of resettling such massive numbers of people? The Dives syndrome is alive and well among modern people.

Ultimately, in the US, both Democrats and Republicans came together to say, "We must accept these people. This is the right and humane thing to do." The Canadians said the same. Churches said the same.

I was a sophomore in high school when some of these Vietnamese of Chinese descent moved into our community and became a part of our lives. Ultimately Canada welcomed overone hundred thousand and the US welcomed over four hundred thousand. The politicians, churches, and communities saw Lazarus. They looked at the Hoa people—a people who were desperate and needed compassion—and they chose to welcome them, to welcome the stranger. When Gladwell asked his mother's friends why they had welcomed the boat people, they responded by reciting the words of Jesus in Matthew 25, "I was a stranger and you welcomed me."

In that season, in America and Canada, Lady Liberty's poem on her pedestal rang true:

> "Give me your tired, your poor,
> Your huddled masses yearning to breathe free,
> The wretched refuse of your teeming shore.
> Send these, the homeless, tempest-tost to me,
> I lift my lamp beside the golden door!"

Do you remember the name of the poet who penned those words in 1883, words that were placed on the Statue of Liberty in 1903? Her name was Emma *Lazarus*.

We have a choice every day: we can ignore Lazarus as Dives did. Or we can see the people like Lazarus we encounter and offer help, as the Good Samaritan did for the man left for dead on the side of the road. Dives or Good Samaritan—which will you be?

4

ON THE JOURNEY TO JERUSALEM

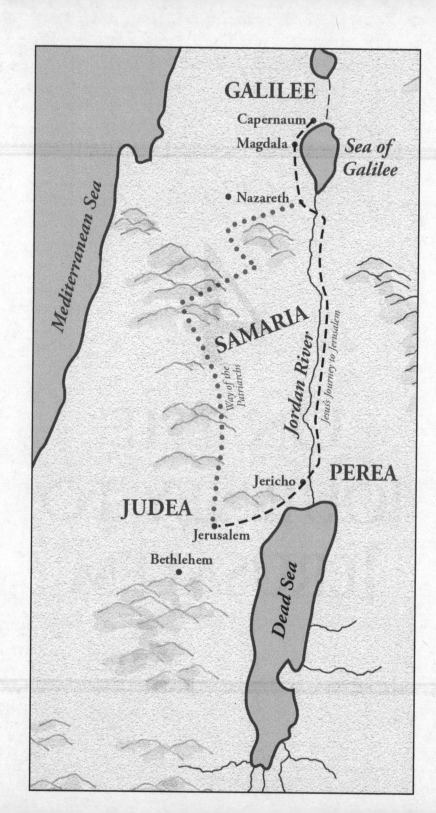

4

ON THE JOURNEY
TO JERUSALEM

As the time approached when Jesus was to be taken up into heaven, he determined to go to Jerusalem. He sent messengers on ahead of him. Along the way, they entered a Samaritan village to prepare for his arrival, but the Samaritan villagers refused to welcome him because he was determined to go to Jerusalem.

(Luke 9:51-53)

Forty percent of Luke's Gospel, ten chapters, has as its setting Jesus's journey to Jerusalem that will end in his death. This begins at Luke 9:51, where Jesus "determined to go" to or as the NRSV translates more literally, "he set his face to go" to Jerusalem. This determination or resoluteness emphasizes that Jesus knows what his disciples do not yet understand: death awaits him in Jerusalem.

In Luke 9:22-25 (NRSV), Jesus attempted to prepare them for this journey and its climax at Calvary:

"The Son of Man must undergo great suffering, and be rejected by the elders, chief priests, and scribes, and be killed, and on the third day be raised."

Then he said to them all, "If any want to become my followers, let them deny themselves, and take up their cross daily and follow me. For those who want to save their life will lose it, and those who lose their life for my sake will save it. What does it profit them if they gain the whole world, but lose or forfeit themselves?"

61

Once more we see the reversal of fortunes. The Son of Man must suffer, be rejected, and die, *but* he will be raised on the third day. Any who want to follow Jesus must deny themselves, be willing to sacrifice themselves daily, and follow him. The one who wishes to save his life will lose it, *but* those who lose their lives will save them. And what good is it if you gain everything but lose your very self or your soul?

This was undoubtedly perplexing to them and did not align with their expectations for the Messiah, nor for their own lives. Jesus sometimes said things that didn't make sense to them, but they could at least hear Christ's call to self-denial, the reminder that you can gain the world and lose your soul. Nine days later, Jesus "determined to go to Jerusalem."

I'd like to say a couple of words about the journey first, then we'll focus on a couple of stories from the journey.

Not a Linear Journey

If you trace out on a map the journey from the Galilee to Jerusalem, what Luke describes is hard to make sense of. Take a look at the map on page 60. There are various ways to divide up the Holy Land of Jesus's time, but one is simply to divide it into three parts from north to south. The northernmost part was the Galilee. Jesus grew up and spent most of his life and ministry in this region. Galilee included a large population of Jews but also foreigners. The center of the country was Samaria, home to the Samaritans and roughly equivalent to the West Bank, home to the Palestinians today. And the south was Judea. Jesus was born there, in Bethlehem. He was baptized in Judea, near Jericho. And he would be arrested, crucified, buried, and resurrected in Jerusalem.

There were two main routes to get from the Galilee to Jerusalem. Regardless of which you took, it would have taken five to nine days depending upon stops and your pace. Yet ten chapters of Luke are devoted to this journey. As you follow where Jesus is during these chapters, it does not appear to make chronological or geographical sense. But if you understand that from Luke 9:51 on, the Crucifixion and his journey to Jerusalem are always on Jesus's mind, this journey makes more sense.

Luke uses this context of Jesus's final journey, I believe, to heighten the sense of urgency of his teaching, and the importance of the ministry that takes place here.

Much of Jesus's teaching takes place on this journey. We've already delved into part of that teaching in the last chapter. Knowing he was on his way to be crucified, the parables we just studied take on greater meaning as we realize that Jesus is thinking about his death in Jerusalem as he teaches each day. I think we might see the stories that take place on the journey in this light as well.

Consider the story of Mary and Martha that we looked at in chapter 2. That event took place on this final journey. Once we know that Jesus is on his way to be crucified, does that change how we read Jesus's words to Martha, "Martha, Martha, you are worried and distracted by many things. One thing is necessary. Mary has chosen the better part. It won't be taken away from her" (Luke 10:41-42)? To me, knowing that Jesus is preparing for his death, these words take on a deeper meaning and sense of urgency, as if to say, "This *really* matters."

Let's briefly consider the things Jesus does and teaches on this final journey.

Lessons from Jesus's Final Journey

In Luke 10, Jesus sends out seventy-two disciples to the towns and villages of the region, commissioning them to "heal the sick who are there, and say to them, 'God's kingdom has come upon you'" (verse 9). The story raises questions: Who are these additional sixty disciples? Where did they come from? They must have been following Jesus. Were some of them the women we've learned about following him? We don't know. But what we see is Jesus preparing them for his departure. The day will come when he will no longer be with them. This is his succession plan: He sends them out in pairs, without him, and he tells them to do what they've seen him doing. He's getting them ready for his death. When they return, he celebrates what they have done, encourages them, and tells them he has given them his authority over "all the power of the enemy" (verse 19).

It is here in Luke 10 that Jesus makes clear what the two great commandments are, shares the parable of the good Samaritan, and eats with Martha and Mary. It is on this journey, in chapter 11, that Jesus teaches his disciples the Lord's Prayer.

But it is also here, on the journey, that the conflict and tension grow between himself and his opponents. In chapter 11, some in the crowd, presumably the religious leaders, claim that Jesus casts out demons not by God's power but by the power of the prince of demons, Beelzebul. I have had people say hurtful things about me over time. I'm guessing you have too. But I wonder what it felt like to be Jesus, God with us, healing the sick and casting out demons, and to have some in the crowd say that you were operating by the power of Beelzebul.

Perhaps this is why Jesus's tone begins to change. Or perhaps it is simply the fact that Jesus is on his way to Jerusalem to be put to death at the behest of some of these religious leaders, and that his time is short, that Jesus becomes harsh with the religious leaders and their rules.

Look at Luke 11:37-54. The Pharisees criticize Jesus for not ritually washing his hands as their rules required (Luke 11:37-38). In response, Jesus unleashes a series of critiques that were quite harsh, as if to say, Really? You're upset that I didn't pour the cup of water over my hands for ritual purity before I eat? Listen, "You

Pharisees clean the outside of the cup and platter, but your insides are stuffed with greed and wickedness. Foolish people! Didn't the one who made the outside also make the inside? Therefore, give to those in need from the core of who you are and you will be clean all over" (Luke 11:39-41).

This is actually the gentlest of the comments Jesus makes to them. Notice his line of reasoning. You are worried about ritually purifying your hands so that nothing sinful or dirty goes into you while you eat. But you don't care about the unclean thoughts, your selfishness and self-righteousness that are on the inside! It would be like, he says, washing the outside of a cup but not the inside. Then he offers this one little line that touches on what we learned in the last chapter, "Give to those in need from the core of who you are and you will be clean all over" (11:41). The act of generosity to the poor actually serves to cleanse our hearts and souls? Yes, in that act we lift up the lowly, we become instruments of God. We deny ourselves and take up our cross.

By chapter 12, a crowd of "thousands upon thousands" have gathered to hear Jesus. Why here and now? And who is this crowd? It seems likely it is, once more, the *'Am ha-Arez*, the uncouth, the "bumpkins," the uneducated and the unobservant who were, nonetheless, hungry for God. Remember we learned from Kauffman Kohler's article in the *Jewish Encyclopedia* of the antipathy between the Pharisees and the *'Am ha-Arez* that led many of them to be drawn to Jesus. Rabbi Akiva ben Yosef, who lived from around AD 50 to 135, once said, "When I was one of the uneducated [another way of speaking of the *'Am ha-Arez*], I used to say, 'Give me one of the learned scribes that I may bite him like an ass'"![1] Clearly, the common people were frustrated with the religious elite.

Jesus goes on to say, "Watch out for the yeast of the Pharisees—I mean, the mismatch between their hearts and lives" (12:1b). He tells them to not be afraid of those who can kill the body, but instead to fear the One who controls your eternal fate. Then he comforts his disciples and the thousands more who are listening, "Aren't five sparrows sold for two small coins? Yet not one of them is overlooked by God. Even the hairs on your head are all counted. Don't be afraid. You are worth more than many sparrows" (Luke 12:6-7). The backdrop to these sayings is the journey Jesus is on and the destiny that awaits him.

Sometimes when I preach, I am preaching to me before I'm preaching to anyone else. I wonder if Jesus, as he is saying these things, is not only comforting his disciples but reminding himself that he need not be afraid, because even the hairs of his head are numbered.

> ## "One's life isn't determined by one's possessions, even when someone is very wealthy." (Luke 12:15)

It is in the context of this journey that Jesus teaches about money and possessions, "Watch out! Guard yourself against all kinds of greed. After all, one's life isn't determined by one's possessions, even when someone is very wealthy" (Luke 12:15). And, once more, he speaks of caring for the poor (the lowly), "Sell your possessions and give to those in need. Make for yourselves wallets that don't wear out—a treasure in heaven that never runs out. No thief comes near there, and no moth destroys. Where your treasure is, there your heart will be too" (12:33-34).

I'm skimming these chapters—I hope you'll read them on your own—there's so much power in the words Jesus teaches on this journey.

Take a look at Luke 13:10-17. Jesus is in a synagogue on the Sabbath. The rabbis had rules about what you could and could not do on the Sabbath, but Jesus sees a powerless and infirm woman there, feeble and frail, bent over. She'd been disabled, Luke says, "by a spirit for eighteen years." "When he saw her, Jesus called her to him and said, 'Woman, you are set free from your sickness.' He placed his hands on her and she straightened up at once and praised God" (verses 12-13). Can I tell you how much I love this picture of Jesus? He knows what he's about to do is against the rules. Furthermore, he is in the synagogue and there is a religious leader there! But he cannot help himself. This woman has been in pain for eighteen years. This is one of the things I hope you will remember about Jesus: *Jesus put people ahead of rules.* The synagogue leader is undone and he chastises this woman and the crowd around, "There are six days during which work is permitted. Come and be healed on those days, not on the Sabbath day" (verse 14). I'll let you read Jesus's response in Luke 13:15-16 and how the crowd responded in verse 17.

Notice, though, that he *saw* the woman. Notice that he had compassion for her. Notice that he refused to let her suffer anymore, Sabbath or not.

Take a look at verse 30 where Jesus articulates the great reversal in the clearest way he could, "Look! Those who are last will be first and those who are first will be last."

Turn to Luke 14, where once more Jesus articulates the attitude God seeks of his people. He's sitting at another of those dinners a Pharisee is hosting for him. This says that Jesus hasn't totally alienated the Pharisees just yet. There are still some who are fascinated by him. Or are they hosting him in order to trap him? The dinner opens with another test about healing on the sabbath, showing once more Jesus's compassion for the sick. But it is what happens next that I want you to notice.

"Jesus noticed how the guests sought out the best seats at the table." The fact that today most committed Christians routinely try to take the lesser seats, the seats on the end of the table where you can't hear so well, or the seats with your back to the stage, or the seats with the odd cousin no one else wants to sit with, is because we know this parable. Even so, we know which seats we want. We want front row center. We want to sit at the "cool kids' table." Jesus tells a parable about a wedding and then says, "All who lift themselves up will be brought low, and those who make themselves low will be lifted up" (Luke 14:11). I'm reminded again that Jesus sought out "friends in low places."

Remember, as we learned in the last chapter, that Luke 15 begins, "All the tax collectors and sinners were gathering around Jesus to listen to him. The Pharisees and legal experts were grumbling, saying, 'This man welcomes sinners and eats with them.'" He goes on to tell them the parables of the lost sheep, the lost coin, and the lost boy—all expressing the heart of God for those who have "wandered from the fold of God" and God's joy when someone who had wandered away comes back to him again. He loves the outsider, the outcast, and the outlaw.

I don't know how that resonates with your heart, but it fills my heart with joy when I think about this. It gives me hope, personally, for the many ways I fall short of God's will. It gives me hope for the people I know and love who are not yet following Christ—that he loves them like the shepherd loves the one lost sheep and like the father loves the prodigal son. But it also fills my heart with joy that the God that we love and serve, who came to us in Jesus, has a heart like this for sinners and tax collectors, for the lost and the broken, for the people who have wandered from him. And it reminds me what churches are to be like, the welcome they are meant to give, the people they are meant to love.

Lepers:
The Ultimate Outsiders and Outcasts

What the Common English Bible and other translations call "skin disease" is the Greek word *lepra*, which is usually translated "leprosy." This could have applied to a wide array of skin diseases and even to molds that grew on the walls of homes or clothing. Leprosy proper, what is usually called Hansen's disease, can cause lesions on the body and physical deformities. While biblical leprosy may have included other, less serious illnesses, it included this form of leprosy as well. People were terrified of contracting leprosy, and it is easy to see how those diagnosed as lepers became instant outcasts and outsiders, especially in light of the biblical laws concerning skin disease. We read in Leviticus 13:45-46:

> *Anyone with an infection of skin disease must wear torn clothes, dishevel their hair, cover their upper lip, and shout out, "Unclean! Unclean!" They will be unclean as long as they are infected. They are unclean. They must live alone outside the camp.*

These "lepers" were literally outcasts, as skin disease in the first century forced people to live as outsiders. Many of us received a small taste of this during COVID-19. The first time LaVon and I had COVID-19 was the week of Christmas 2020. A neighbor suggested I tie a ribbon on my tree so that my neighbors would know to keep their distance. LaVon had it first. She stayed quarantined in a bedroom upstairs while I brought food to her door (she was unwilling to let me come in, for fear of infecting me). Four or five days after she tested positive, I tested positive. On Christmas Day, our kids stood outside the garage door to wish us Merry Christmas, our first Christmas ever to not spend the day together. We spoke to them from fifteen feet away. This was a very minor experience of being outcasts compared with the lepers of Jesus's day, who were isolated from their family and friends with a disease that could have terrifying results. They were ostracized and lived without the touch of another human.

Luke contains two stories of Jesus healing lepers, and a reference to others. The first is in Luke 5:12-13:

> *Jesus was in one of the towns where there was also a man covered with a skin disease. When he saw Jesus, he fell on his face and begged, "Lord, if you want, you can make me clean."*
>
> *Jesus reached out, touched him, and said, "I do want to. Be clean." Instantly, the skin disease left him.*

I love that Jesus responds to the man's words, "If you want, you can make me clean," by saying "I do *want* to." But I also love that small detail, "Jesus reached out, touched him…" Jesus could have simply said the word and the man would have been made well, but he insisted on touching him, something this man may not have felt—another human's touch—since being diagnosed with leprosy.

In the late 1980s, as a young associate pastor, I went to the hospital to visit one of the members of the congregation I was serving. He had AIDS and was dying. This was a time when a great deal of fear surrounded HIV/AIDS. Though medical scientists had been clear that HIV was not spread through casual touch or being in proximity with someone who had AIDS, I admit I felt some anxiety as I entered his room. It was this story of Jesus touching the leper that was on my mind as I sat down next to him and took his hand. We sat together as he told me his story, and I told him of Christ's love for him. Before I left, I anointed his forehead with oil, in the sign of the cross, and committed his life to Christ.

Touch matters. Whenever I visit the hospital, my hope is to incarnate the love of Christ, and holding a person's hand is one way to do that. Not everyone will want you to hold their hand. And there are some situations which will require that touch be through latex gloves to prevent the spread of an infectious disease. But for most people, touch is important. "Jesus reached out and touched him…" As I left the hospital room, the patient with AIDS squeezed my hand as if to say, "thank you for holding my hand."

The Samaritans

You undoubtedly know that there was bad blood between the Jews and Samaritans. The animosity had existed for hundreds of years. I don't have space to recount the history here. Second Kings 17 will give you a sense of how Jews in the time 2 Kings was compiled viewed the Samaritans. In many ways this relationship is similar to the Jewish-Palestinian relationship today, including the fact that the Palestinian West Bank sets roughly where Samaria was located in the ancient world.

Samaritans were treated by many Jews as unclean and second class. Jews saw the Samaritans as foreigners, or at best mixed race, not true Israelites. They saw the Samaritan faith as defective and their lives as impure. The Pharisees and religiously devout would have attempted to avoid associating with Samaritans. The Samaritans felt this disdain, the sense that they were outsiders and outcasts. But the Samaritans had developed their own response to the Jewish disdain. They said that the Jews were not true Jews. They held that when the Babylonians had taken the Jewish people captive in the sixth century BC, the Jewish faith became distorted by their sojourn in Babylon. That they, the Samaritans, were the true Israelites, not the Jews.

There were people among both the Jews and Samaritans who did not embrace this conflict, and who sought to treat one another as neighbors and friends. But the stories in the Gospels make clear that this was the exception not the rule.

For Jews living in the Galilee, who sought to make their way to Jerusalem for the high holy days, this conflict was seen in the route they took. The fastest way to Jerusalem from most places in the Galilee was the Way of Patriarchs, which ran right through Samaria. But many Jews would not take this route, either for fear of the Samaritans or simply to avoid contact with them. Instead, they would journey southeast, cross the Jordan at a ford south of the Sea of Galilee, and then travel the King's Highway in what is today Jordan before crossing the fords near Jericho.

Are there people who folks in your religion, race, ethnicity, location, or socioeconomic status consciously or subconsciously treat as "less than"?

For you and your community, who are the Samaritans? Who are the Jews? Are there people who act as though you, or people of your religion, race, location, or socioeconomic status are "less than"? Are there people who folks in your religion, race, ethnicity, location, or socioeconomic status consciously or subconsciously treat as less than? Are there neighborhoods or communities or nations you would be afraid to travel through? Are there people who would hesitate to travel through the community where you live?

Our central campus of Resurrection is located in Leawood, Kansas. At one time, in the 1950s, where the city was acquiring more land, it drew its boundaries around an existing neighborhood because there were Jewish families living there. The covenants and restrictions of new neighborhoods back then kept Blacks, Jews, and people of other Semitic backgrounds from moving into the neighborhoods or joining the country clubs that were sprouting up in the area.

Things have changed a lot. These restrictions are no longer legal. They would be unthinkable to most residents of the city today.

But our population remains overwhelmingly white. One of our members, an African American woman, a highly respected federal court judge, described the day she was moving into a neighborhood near the church thirty-two years ago, and how, as her husband was coming in and out of the house loading and unloading boxes, the police stopped to inquire what he was doing, concerned that perhaps there was a theft in progress. Since graduating from seminary, I've moved five times, and I've never had the police stop by to see what I was doing. Fear of the other, stereotypes, and assumptions are hard to legislate away.

That can be true for both sides of the fear, distrust, and disdain equation. As Jesus began his journey to Jerusalem in Luke 9:51, he appeared to plan to make the journey through Samaria. But the first Samaritan village he came to "refused to welcome him because he was determined to go to Jerusalem" (Luke 9:53). The disciples then asked Jesus if they should (or could?) call down fire from heaven to destroy this Samaritan village! Really? Destroy the village because of their fears and their refusal to welcome Jesus? Jesus "spoke sternly" to his disciples, chastising them for such talk. As I read those words the thought struck me, "I wonder what it would feel like to have Jesus speak sternly to you?" I hope to never find out.

Knowing this background is central to understanding the parable of the good Samaritan that we considered in the last chapter. Remember, the Jewish lawyer had asked Jesus, "What must I do to inherit eternal life?" Jesus turns the question on the man, asking, "What is written in the Law? How do you interpret it?" The man rightly recited what Jesus elsewhere described as the two great commandments, the love of God and neighbor. And the man, as you recall, asked one more question, "Who is my neighbor?" It was then that Jesus told the parable of the good Samaritan (Luke 10:25-37).

In that story, after a "certain man" on his way from Jerusalem to Jericho was accosted, robbed, and left for dead, a Jewish priest and a Levite pass by on the other side of the street, avoiding contact with the wounded, or perhaps dead, man. Fear. But along comes a Samaritan. A Samaritan? Yes, a Samaritan. He sees the man who is injured by the side of the road. He has the courage to stop to help the man. He sacrifices and demonstrates love and justice. Jesus makes the Samaritan the hero of the story. The one Jews considered defective in his faith (the Samaritan) is the one who actually loves his neighbor, while the two devout religious leaders fail to do what God requires. I wanted to mention this parable once more here so that we could see what Jesus has done. While teaching on the border of the Galilee and Samaria, even after a Samaritan village refused to allow him to stay, he has portrayed the Samaritan as the righteous man. He has undermined the assumptions and stereotypes of the Jews who are hearing him speak.

A Lesson from
the Samaritan Leper

With all this talk of lepers and Samaritans, we're now ready to consider Luke 17. Eight chapters have passed while Jesus was on his journey, and he's seemingly made almost no progress. He's right where he began, still traveling along the border of Samaria. Here's how the story begins in Luke 17:11-13:

> On the way to Jerusalem, Jesus traveled along the border between Samaria and Galilee. As he entered a village, ten men with skin diseases approached him. Keeping their distance from him, they raised their voices and said, "Jesus, Master, show us mercy!"

While entering a border town, he encounters not one, but ten lepers. You know how lepers were ostracized, in some ways the ultimate outcast. These men longed to be healed and to return to their community. Notice, they *raised their voices* and pleaded with Jesus, "*Show us mercy!*" The word *mercy* here is, in Greek, *eleeson*. You may recognize it if you come from a Catholic, Eastern Orthodox, or liturgical Protestant background, as you've likely prayed or chanted *Kyrie Eleison*—Lord, have mercy. It is sung or spoken as part of the mass. Or perhaps you know it from the 1985 Mr. Mister song by the same name, or the later Chris Tomlin song.

I wonder if you ever find yourself without words to pray except "Lord, have mercy!" You'll remember it was the prayer of the tax collector who prayed as he beat his breast, head bowed down, "God, show mercy to me, a sinner." These ten outcasts cried out with this same plea to Jesus. Mercy is undeserved kindness, compassion, help. Master, have mercy on us! Lord, Jesus, have mercy on me. I am listening to Mr. Mister's 1985 "Live at the Ritz in NYC" music video (Google it) as I'm writing these words, "Kyrie eleison down the road that I must travel." That is a magnificent daily prayer. It is a powerful prayer when you don't know what to say. Lord, have mercy.

Note what happens next. Luke writes, "When Jesus saw them, he said, 'Go, show yourselves to the priests.' As they left, they were cleansed" (17:14). Notice once more that Jesus *saw them*. Jesus sees those that others treat as invisible or hope to ignore. He sees us when we feel unseen. He saw them in their pain and suffering and alienation. Unlike the leper in Luke 5, this time Jesus did not touch the lepers. They remained at a distance. He simply spoke and they were made well.

The story hearkens back to the story of Elisha the prophet and Naaman, the commander of Syria's army, in 2 Kings 5. Naaman was a foreigner, a general, who came to the Israelite prophet asking for him to deliver him from his leprosy. Rather than touching him or giving him some medicinal treatment, Elisha speaks, telling Naaman to go wash in the Jordan River and he would be made clean. This act required Naaman to trust in God and also in Elisha's words. He was offended at first, but ultimately did what Elisha said and was made well. Jesus's healing of these ten lepers didn't happen instantaneously.

He told them to go find the priest—the biblical requirement for a leper who had been healed. Jesus told them this before they were healed, and the act of going to find the priest would be an act of faith. On the way, they were healed.

So we see once more Jesus's concern for the outcast and outsider. But that is not the end of this story. The denouement—the closing scene that brings out the final, or perhaps most important, point—is yet to come:

> One of them, when he saw that he had been healed, returned and praised God **with a loud voice**. He **fell on his face** at Jesus' feet and **thanked him**. He was **a Samaritan**. Jesus replied, "Weren't ten cleansed? Where are the other nine? No one returned to praise God except this foreigner?" Then Jesus said to him, "Get up and go. Your faith has healed you."
>
> (Luke 17:15-17, emphasis added)

Here the story shifts from Jesus's compassion to one leper's gratitude. This *Samaritan* leper becomes the hero of the story, as in the parable of the good Samaritan. This event happens on the border between Galilee and Samaria. We don't know which side of the dividing line the village is in. We already know in reading Luke's Gospel that Jesus can and wants to heal lepers. But here the Samaritan leper helps us learn that the appropriate response to Jesus, to his love and grace, his friendship and mercy, his lifting up the lowly, is gratitude.

There are two words that summarize the heart of the Christian response to God: thank you. These two words describe the essence of Christian worship. They help us understand how we are meant to live our lives. But how hard it is to remember them. We try to teach our children, every time someone does something kind for them, to express gratitude. "What do you say?" we ask, and they say, "Thank you." But why do we need to remind them? And who is reminding us?

There are two words that summarize the heart of the Christian response to God: thank you.

Ten lepers were set free that day. They would no longer be outcasts. They would be welcomed back to their homes and communities. Nine were undoubtedly celebrating. Only one realized that the most important thing he needed to do was to "praise God with a loud voice," to fall "on his face at Jesus' feet," and to thank him. And this man who got it right, who reminded us what it means to be faithful and what it means to be human, "was a Samaritan." Once more Luke wants us to see the lowly lifted up; and, despite what the Jews near Samaria thought, he wanted us to see who the righteous man really was.

As with the parables, we're meant in hearing this story to ask, "Am I more like the nine, or like the Samaritan?" I have often been more like the nine—whenever the crisis has passed and I'm on to the next thing, and I have completely forgotten to fall at Jesus's feet and to express my gratitude for all Christ has done for me or for the people I have prayed for.

How are your knees? Try falling on them today—right now if you can—and stop to give thanks for all that Christ has done for you. Daily give thanks. The Samaritan leper, like the Samaritan in the parable, becomes a model for the Christian spiritual life. It is not rocket science. Pay attention to the needs of people around you. *See* them. Help them. Cry out to Jesus for mercy on the road that you must travel. Trust him. And give thanks.

As I was completing the final revisions of this chapter, I received a call that someone I deeply care about was in the hospital and having some heart issues. Fear was a very real response. As we talked, I began to talk to him about this story. Three things I suggested he might hold on to as he was alone in the hospital: the first was the prayer of the ten lepers: Jesus, Master, have mercy. I mentioned, "When you start to feel afraid, simply whisper it as a breath prayer: Jesus, Master, have mercy on me." Second was to remember that when Jesus told the lepers to go show themselves to the priests, they still had leprosy. They had to have faith and to trust that Jesus was somehow at work even though they could not see it. I told my friend, "Trust that he's there in the hospital room when you feel you are all alone. Trust that he's going to work through the doctors and the treatment plan. Let him know, Jesus, I trust you with my life. And finally, like the Samaritan leper, praise God and give thanks to Jesus."

The Journey Nears Its End

There are two final passages I'd like to encourage you to look at as we prepare to move to Jerusalem for the final week of Jesus's life, passages I don't want you to miss on the journey Jesus is making. The first is Jesus's teaching about God's kingdom. After Jesus heals the lepers, the Pharisees, who after all of this are still following Jesus around, ask him, "When is God's kingdom coming?" (Luke 17:20, paraphrased). Jesus's response is this, "Don't you see? God's kingdom is already among you" (Luke 17:21). He says more, following this, about the judgment to come. But this line is one worth pondering: "The kingdom of God is among you." The kingdom of God is not merely some future state, though there is a future dimension to it. The kingdom or reign of God is in your midst as you follow Jesus, as you see all the people who need his love and grace, as you show compassion for the hurting, the broken, the outcasts, the outsiders, and the outlaws, and as you lift up the lowly. When you do this, when you not only pray, but act to see God's will be done, you are a part of bringing the kingdom of God on earth as it is in heaven.

The second passage is a story that Luke tells as Jesus draws near to Jericho. It's a familiar one found in Luke 18:15-17 and captures, once more, Jesus's love for the lowly:

People were bringing babies to Jesus so that he would bless them. When the disciples saw this, they scolded them. Then Jesus called them to him and said, "Allow the children to come to me. Don't forbid them, because God's kingdom belongs to people like these children. I assure you that whoever doesn't welcome God's kingdom like a child will never enter it."

What a great picture of Jesus! Parents want Jesus to bless their children, the very thing I've prayed every day for thirty-five years since our oldest, Danielle, was born. Every day, several times a day, I name my children, their spouses, and now my granddaughter, to Jesus, asking for his arms to enfold them, for his blessing upon them, his guiding hand to lead them. These parents were seeking what I seek daily. But the disciples see these parents coming to Jesus with their infants and they think, "Jesus is too busy and far too important to be troubled with blessing babies!"

When the journey began, he chastised his disciples for wanting to call down fire on the Samaritan village that refused him. Now he corrects his disciples for scolding these parents saying (in the King James Version, which I love), "Suffer little children to come unto me, and forbid them not: for of such is the kingdom of God" (Matthew 19:14).

From this and other passages we learn to sing, "Jesus loves the little children, all the children of the world...." Here we learn his heart for the utterly powerless and helpless. I love how New Testament scholar David Garland says of this passage, "Jesus consistently sides with those on the fringe and considered expendable—the least, those who have no rights, those held cheap by others. The new community he founds [the church—your church and my church] embraces the little ones rather than banishing them."[2] Then Garland quotes another scholar, Father Joseph Fitzmyer in his commentary on this passage, "To receive a little child is to accept and esteem even the lowliest of human society."[3]

What are you and your church doing to welcome and bless children? How are you honoring the Samaritans and caring for the lepers? In what ways are you putting people before rules?

5
THE FINAL WEEK

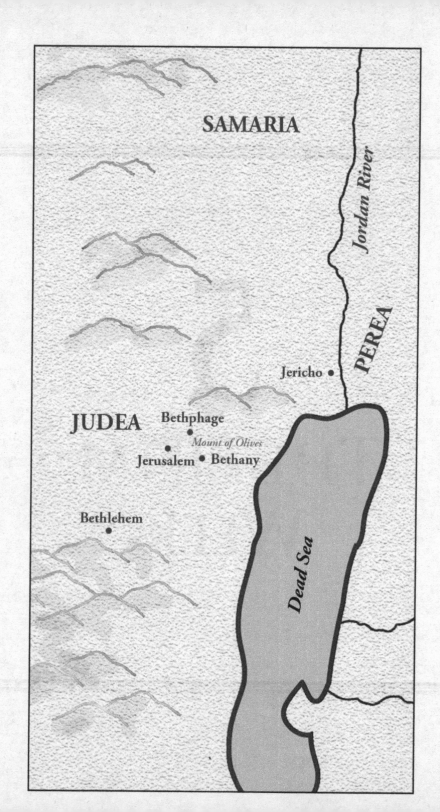

5

THE FINAL WEEK

All who saw it began to grumble and said, "He has gone to be the guest of one who is a sinner." Zacchaeus stood there and said to the Lord, "Look, half of my possessions, Lord, I will give to the poor; and if I have defrauded anyone of anything, I will pay back four times as much." Then Jesus said to him, "Today salvation has come to this house, because he too is a son of Abraham. For the Son of Man came to seek out and to save the lost."

(Luke 19:7-10 NRSV)

[At the Last Supper] an argument broke out among the disciples over which one of them should be regarded as the greatest.

But Jesus said to them, "The kings of the Gentiles rule over their subjects, and those in authority over them are called 'friends of the people.' But that's not the way it will be with you. Instead the greatest among you must become like a person of lower status and the leader like a servant. So which one is greater, the one who is seated at the table or the one who serves at the table? Isn't it the one who is seated at the table? But I am among you as one who serves."

(Luke 22:24-27)

If you knew you only had one week to live, where would you go? Who would you spend time with? What would you say and do? As we come to the end of Luke 18, this is, in fact, what Jesus knows: in a week, he'll be put to death in Jerusalem.

In this chapter, we'll turn to the final week of Jesus's life and the things he said and did on the days leading up to his crucifixion. Each word and story express what matters most to Jesus. Let's consider a few of the events and some of the conversations and interactions Jesus has with others during his final week.

Two Rich Men and a Blind Beggar

As Jesus prepared to enter Jericho, "A certain ruler asked Jesus, 'Good Teacher, what must I do to obtain eternal life?'" (Luke 18:18). This is the second time someone has asked Jesus this question in Luke. The first was the religious lawyer to whom Jesus told the parable of the good Samaritan, in which the Samaritan stops to help a man beaten and left for dead. He selflessly cares for him and provides for his needs. That is part of what it looks like to inherit eternal life.

In the case of the ruler who approaches Jesus outside of Jericho, Jesus responds to the man's question by reciting five of the Ten Commandments: "Don't commit adultery. Don't murder. Don't steal. Don't give false testimony. Honor your father and mother." The man replied, "I've kept all these things since I was a boy" (Luke 18:20-21). I love how Mark tells us that, at this point, "Jesus looked at him carefully and loved him" (Mark 10:21).

Jesus then gives him one more command, a command that has left his disciples uneasy ever since: "There's one more thing. Sell everything you own and distribute the money to the poor. Then you will have treasure in heaven. And come, follow me" (Luke 18:22). Yikes! This was certainly not what the wealthy ruler expected Jesus to say. Matthew and Mark say that, upon hearing this, the man went away sorrowful for he had many possessions. Luke tells us only that he was very sad for he was extremely rich. Luke goes on to note that Jesus looked at the sad, rich ruler and said, "It's very hard for the wealthy to enter God's kingdom! It's easier for a camel to squeeze through the eye of a needle than for a rich person to enter God's kingdom" (Luke 18:24-25).

(By the way, this is now the third time Jesus has said, in Luke's Gospel, that we are to sell what we have and give to the poor. The three are Luke 12:33, 14:33, and here in 18:22. We cannot merely say that this command was only for this particular rich ruler.)

Luke continues, "Those who heard this said, 'Then who can be saved?'" (verse 26). In Matthew it is the disciples who utter this question. In Luke and Mark it is the crowd. Then Jesus offers a lifeline, "What is impossible for humans is possible for God" (verse 27). In other words, we are saved by God's grace, as Paul notes in Ephesians 2:8-9, not by our works. Thank God, there's hope. But that does not mean we can dismiss this seemingly impossible ideal Jesus has just given to this rich ruler, and through him, to us.

Let's recognize that this saying of Jesus is troubling for almost everyone. And I think that is precisely what Jesus intended. It is good for us to be troubled. We are *supposed to struggle with these words.*

When I consider this passage, I am struck by the contradictions. It would seem to be literally impossible for most of us to sell *all* that we possess and give it to the poor. We would find ourselves poor, naked, homeless, and hungry, counting on someone who still owned things to supply our needs. If the world's two billion Christians did this, it would be a humanitarian and economic crisis of epic proportions. Our global economy, people's jobs, are built upon providing goods and services. It simply doesn't work if everyone is selling all they possess, giving to the poor, and living homeless. Even those who have tried ended up owning possessions. The homeless themselves typically have a knapsack, bag, or shopping cart with their possessions. There is no food without farmers who own tractors and implements and land to farm. I've been to some of the poorest countries on earth, and people there still have mud brick huts, sheep, and clothing. Increasingly they have cell phones, they have tools by which they create, and they sustain themselves by selling and buying.

Jesus himself had clothes and shoes. He ate in people's homes without chastising them for owning a home where they could feed him. The women who followed him had money with which they provided food and other supplies for the disciples. This feels like it is an ideal that is not entirely possible but is meant to shape what is possible and how we do live, even if we don't fully live this way.

It helps me to remember that Jesus often spoke in hyperbole: "If your right eye causes you to fall into sin, tear it out and throw it away.... And if your right hand causes you to fall into sin, chop it off and throw it away" (Matthew 5:29-30). If we applied this literally, we'd all be blind and missing our right hands. But that is not what Jesus was looking for when he spoke those words. He was looking to shake us up and say, "Sin is serious business. Stop it!" I think this is what Jesus was after in the command to the rich ruler.

You are the means by which God lifts up the lowly and ensures the hungry go home full.

If Jesus did not intend for us to take this command completely literally, then how are we to take it? I think he's saying, You don't need most of what you want or already have. Simplify. Stop being driven by the acquisition of more. It is a false god. Your life does not consist in the abundance of your possessions. You cannot serve both God and money, so choose God instead of money. To whom much is given, much more is expected. God expects you to be generous. Give and it will be given to you, pressed down, shaken together, and running over—the blessings of God come when you are generous toward others. And, perhaps most important, you are the means by which God lifts up the lowly and ensures the hungry go home full.

I need these words of Jesus, even if they disturb me. Though I will never measure up to the command Jesus gave the rich ruler, his giving this command has changed my relationship with money and how I spend it. It has moved me to rethink "how much is enough?" And it has led me to greater generosity and compassion than I would ever have pursued without these words.

A Blind Beggar Is Healed

After his encounter with the rich man (Luke 18:18-22), Jesus sets up the week that's ahead. He took the Twelve aside and said to them:

> *"See, we are going up to Jerusalem, and everything that is written about the Son of Man by the prophets will be accomplished. For he will be handed over to the Gentiles; and he will be mocked and insulted and spat upon. After they have flogged him, they will kill him, and on the third day he will rise again." But they understood nothing about all these things; in fact, what he said was hidden from them, and they did not grasp what was said.*
>
> *(Luke 18:31-34 NRSV)*

This is what is on Jesus's mind as he enters Jericho. His heart is heavy. He is preoccupied with the suffering that is coming. Yet, despite the cares that weigh him down, surrounded by a crowd of people, he is still focused on lifting up the lowly.

Luke writes:

> *As Jesus came to Jericho, a certain blind man was sitting beside the road begging. When the man heard the crowd passing by, he asked what was happening. They told him, "Jesus the Nazarene is passing by."*
>
> *The blind man shouted, "Jesus, Son of David, show me mercy." Those leading the procession scolded him, telling him to be quiet, but he shouted even louder, "Son of David, show me mercy."*
>
> *(Luke 18:35-39)*

Beggars can be persistent. This man has undoubtedly been begging for alms on this street, or another like it in Jericho, for a long time. As he hears that Jesus is walking by, he calls out with a royal title, "Jesus, Son of David, show me mercy." Son of David is a title that appears only here in Luke's Gospel. It was a messianic title. It is a blind beggar who is the first to call Jesus by this title in the Gospel. And notice what he asks for: "Show me mercy." Once more I'm reminded of *Kyrie Eleison*—Lord, have mercy. Lord, show me kindness I don't deserve. Come and help me. As the disciples chastised the parents who brought their children to Jesus to be blessed, so here the crowd chastises the blind beggar, "Jesus doesn't need to be bothered with the likes of you!"

Sometimes, when I come to the street corner where different men sit each day with their cardboard signs, I talk to them, ask their names, and give them money, knowing that I don't know how the money will be used, but trying to imitate Jesus. Other times, I think, "I helped the last three guys, you are out of luck," and I look ahead and pretend not to see this person.

One of our members used to be one of those guys. Today he's married and has a job and is doing well. I asked him once, "Knowing what you know as someone who was homeless and holding up the signs, what's the right thing to do? Do we stop and help, or is this one of those cases of 'toxic charity' where helping actually hurts, keeping people dependent?" He responded, "I don't know the answer. I do know that when I was standing out there in the heat or the cold, I was grateful when someone actually rolled down their window, spoke to me, and gave me a few dollars. That's why I stop and give them something."

Mark actually gives a name to the man (Luke only tells us he is a "certain beggar"). Matthew doesn't name him either, but for Matthew, there are two blind beggars there, not one! But Mark tells us his name is Bartimaeus. When I stop at the corner, I always ask their names, and speak to them by name, and try to offer kindness with whatever sum of money I give, and, as I drive away, I pray for them by name. There is something important about learning a person's name and calling a person by name.

The crowd is scolding the man, trying to hush him. Luke continues, "Jesus stopped and called for the man to be brought to him. When he was present Jesus asked, 'What do you want me to do for you?'" Once more, Jesus sees the man, not as a beggar, but as a child of God. Bartimaeus responds, "Lord, I want to see" (verses 40-41).

The story ends, not unlike the healing of the ten lepers, with the blind beggar healed by Jesus. I love Bartimaeus's response: "He began to follow Jesus, praising God" (verse 43). *I once was lost, but now am found, was blind, but now I see.* Did he follow Jesus to Calvary? What was he thinking or feeling as he stood by the cross, seeing the man who opened his eyes being tortured to death at the behest of religious leaders?

A Rich Tax Collector

Few other stories in Luke have had a greater impact on my life than the story of the "wee little man" Zacchaeus. In it Jesus summarizes his mission, both what he'd been doing throughout the Gospel and what he was now preparing to do as he was going into Jerusalem. This story captures once more the contrast between the supposed saints and sinners, between the pious Pharisees and the nonreligious but spiritually hungry *'Am ha-Arez*. Here's how the story begins: "Jesus entered Jericho and was passing through town. A man there named Zacchaeus, a ruler among tax collectors, was rich. He was trying to see who Jesus was, but, being a short man, he couldn't because of the crowd" (Luke 19:1-3).

Zacchaeus is not just a tax collector, he is a *chief* tax collector. The Greek word for ruler or chief is *archon* and it signified a leading and influential person of some standing. By way of reminder, the Roman tax collectors in this period bid on the right to collect taxes—the high bidder would pay the taxes to the Romans up front. Then they would add their commission and expenses to the amount they had paid the Romans and go about trying to collect these taxes from the people. If someone could not or would not pay their taxes, the tax collectors would do whatever they needed to do to collect. Tax collectors were disdained by many of the Jewish people. They were outsiders, considered money-loving, dishonest, and greedy. Zacchaeus was not just a tax collector, he was a *chief* tax collector, which meant that he had others working for him and implied that he was very well off. He is an outsider, an outcast, and an *outlaw* in the eyes of the Jewish people.

Throughout the Gospels, we find that tax collectors were drawn to Jesus. And Jesus, seeing them as outsiders and outcasts, was drawn to reach them. Zacchaeus desperately wanted to see Jesus, but with the crowd gathered around Jesus, he could not see because he was short. I picture Zacchaeus trying to catch a glimpse of Jesus, attempting to push his way to the front, but the people are elbowing him out of the way. There was no love lost between the people of Jericho and Zacchaeus. So, Luke records, "He ran ahead and climbed up a sycamore tree so he could see Jesus, who was about to pass that way" (Luke 19:4).

The story makes me smile, seeing this short—and I picture somewhat overweight—chief tax collector doing what was a rather undignified thing for an adult male to do: climbing a tree to catch a glimpse of Jesus. If you go to Jericho, what many believe is the oldest inhabited city in the world, you'll see they have planted a large sycamore tree in the middle of town where you can climb and reenact this story!

But it's not the small tax collector climbing a tree that has so moved me in this story, it is Jesus's response to him. "When Jesus came to that spot, he looked up and said, '*Zacchaeus, come down at once. I must stay in your home today.*' So Zacchaeus came down at once, happy to welcome Jesus" (Luke 19:5-6, emphasis added). It's as if Jesus has come here to Jericho precisely for this meeting. He walks straight to the sycamore tree and looks up and calls Zacchaeus by name. Jesus already knows this chief tax collector, though they've never met. Jesus has come looking for him. Then Jesus invites himself over with his disciples for the night!

The scene reminds me of Revelation 3:20, where Jesus says, "I'm standing at the door and knocking. If any hear my voice and open the door, I will come in to be with them, and will have dinner with them, and they will have dinner with me." Remember, to eat with someone—to break bread with them—was to be their companion. Jesus seeks to be Zacchaeus's companion. But by implication, this story tells me he wants to be your companion, and mine, and a companion to all of those who don't go to church who see themselves as outsiders or outcasts.

Luke goes on to tell us about the crowd's reaction to Jesus's decision to visit Zacchaeus, as well as Zacchaeus's response: "Everyone who saw this grumbled, saying, 'He has gone to be the guest of a sinner'" (19:7). We see once more the same response to Jesus's ministry and welcome of sinners and tax collectors that we saw in Luke 15:1-2: "All the tax collectors and sinners were gathering around Jesus to listen to him. The Pharisees and legal experts were grumbling, saying, 'This man welcomes sinners and eats with them.'"

It's still hard to imagine that religious people would be grumbling about Jesus spending time with and befriending nonreligious people. Wouldn't you think they would be happy about that? But they didn't see it that way. Jesus must have been "soft on sin." Remember, earlier in Luke, they concluded that Jesus was a glutton and drunkard. They even said he was working for the prince of demons.

But Jesus's embrace of Zacchaeus changed Zacchaeus. His focus in life had been the acquisition of wealth; but listen to how he responded to Jesus's embrace: "Zacchaeus stopped and said to the Lord, 'Look, Lord, I give half of my possessions to the poor. And if I have cheated anyone, I repay them four times as much.'" And Jesus responds, "Today, salvation has come to this household because he too is a son of Abraham" (Luke 19:8-9).

How remarkable is this?! Zacchaeus was not "buying his way to heaven." He was responding to the grace Jesus had shown him.

Let's pause for a moment to see what has happened here. Jesus did not explain the "Roman road to salvation." He did not proclaim to Zacchaeus that he was a sinner and if only he would repent, he would be saved. Jesus did not teach him the deepest truths of the gospel. What did Jesus do? *He called Zacchaeus by name and befriended him.* He showed grace to him and treated him with kindness.

This is part of what we learn from Jesus in this story: *Most people don't become Christ-followers because of our superior theological arguments.* They come to church, and then faith, because someone befriended them and demonstrated the love and acceptance of Christ.

There is a lot of hand-wringing going on today in Christian circles because church membership and worship attendance is dropping in the US. But there is no shortage of people who need to feel they are cared about as human beings, who need to be accepted, befriended, and loved.

Christians have too often become the Pharisees Jesus was pushing against: too quick to judge, to exclude, to leave people feeling not loved, but hurt, as if they were outsiders and outcasts.

Christians have too often become the Pharisees Jesus was pushing against: too quick to judge, to exclude, to leave people feeling not loved, but hurt, as if they were outsiders and outcasts. This is why I love this story.

I picture Jesus going to the home of Zacchaeus that afternoon and Zacchaeus inviting all of his friends over to break bread with Jesus—a house full of nonreligious people. I see the religious people standing outside Zacchaeus's home, grumbling about how the rabbi they thought might be the Messiah was staying in the home of, and eating with, a notorious sinner. It was, I suspect they would say, a disgrace. And in my mind's eye I picture Jesus getting up from the table, walking to the open door of Zacchaeus's home, and approaching one of these religious leaders. I imagine him, jaw clenched, poking the religious leader in the chest and saying, "You just don't get it, do you?" Then, with deep conviction, Jesus says, *"The Son of Man came to seek and to save the lost"* (Luke 19:10 NRSV, emphasis added).

This passage, Luke 19:10, is one I memorized long ago. I have preached it again and again. I share it with everyone interested in joining our church to say, this is what drove Jesus, and it is what drives our church. We are here to be used by God to seek and to save the lost. It is, of course, Jesus who saves them. But we do our part in loving, welcoming, and befriending people as Christ's followers.

Before we leave this story, there is one last thing to notice. Luke places this story shortly after the story of the rich young ruler (Luke 18:18-23). Both the young ruler and Zacchaeus are wealthy. They are both leaders. The young ruler steadfastly kept the law, while Zacchaeus was a tax collector. One was thought to be a saint, the other a sinner. But as we read their stories we're once more forced to ask, which was which?

We look with empathy on the pious ruler who went away sad when Jesus asked him to sell what he had, to give to the poor, and to follow him. I wonder if Zacchaeus was there in the crowd as he heard their conversation? It stands out as remarkable to me that Zacchaeus, who had been a notorious sinner, without being prompted by Jesus, responded to his grace by volunteering to give up half of what he had *for the poor*. He knew there is a connection between our faith, our finances, and our values. In that moment, Zacchaeus was not trying to buy salvation. He was responding to a grace already extended to him.

I know a family in our church who read the story of Zacchaeus, years ago, and decided they wanted to give away an increasing percentage of their income each year. They already gave their first 10 percent to God through the church, an expression of gratitude and praise to God and to support the church's work. But what they gave over that would go to special causes with an emphasis on addressing poverty. After twenty-five years they finally hit their goal, giving 50 percent of their income away. They described to me how they intentionally kept their standard of living fairly level even as their income grew. They told me how much joy they have from being able to make grants and support causes that are making a difference.

I know another family who decided that, while they could not get to 50 percent while they were alive, when they died they wanted to leave 50 percent of their estate to their church and to causes that addressed poverty. The witness of Zacchaeus is still having an impact nearly two thousand years after he welcomed Jesus into his home.

Humble and Riding on a Donkey

After staying the night at Zacchaeus's home, Jesus and the disciples would have left early in the morning to make their way to Jerusalem. The journey is fourteen miles as the crow flies, but it begins at 800 feet below sea level and steadily rises to 2,700 feet above sea level at the top of the Mount of Olives. Parts of the ancient Roman road are still visible to those who hike it today. At a brisk pace the journey could be made in six hours, though at a regular walk, and stopping to rest and for meals, it was likely an eight-hour journey.

If they left Jericho at 8 a.m., shortly after sunrise that spring day, they would have arrived at Bethphage and Bethany on the Mount of Olives early in the afternoon. Once there, Jesus sent two disciples ahead to a village, promising they would find a young donkey "that no one has ever ridden" (Luke 19:30). Jesus asks them to untie it and bring it to him. Jesus has likely prearranged for this donkey as it gives him the chance to make a statement by entering Jerusalem on a donkey.

At no other time in the Gospels does Jesus ride a donkey. Why here? Why now? In requesting the donkey and riding it into Jerusalem, Jesus is giving a clear and recognizable sign that he is the long-awaited Messiah, the King. While anyone might ride a donkey, throughout scripture riding a donkey was associated with royalty. In Genesis 49:11, Jacob speaks to his son Judah promising Judah (and his descendants) will bear the royal scepter and describes him tying "his male donkey to the vine, the colt of his female donkey to the vine's branches." From this verse forward, riding the donkey is associated with royal authority. In a famous incident, King David fled Jerusalem on a donkey. His son and heir, Solomon, later entered the city on a donkey. Hundreds of years before Jesus, the prophet Zechariah foretold that God would send a king who would come riding on a donkey,

> *Rejoice greatly, Daughter Zion.*
> *Sing aloud, Daughter Jerusalem.*
> *Look, your king will come to you.*
> *He is righteous and victorious.*
> *He is humble and riding on an ass,*
> *on a colt, the offspring of a donkey.*
> *(Zechariah 9:9)*

Zechariah also foretells that God will come to his people from the Mount of Olives (Zechariah 14:4). Jesus intentionally "fulfilled" these prophetic words in Zechariah. He was making a clear and dramatic statement regarding his identity as he mounted the donkey to descend the Mount of Olives. He was saying, I am the Messiah, the descendant of David, your King.

But Zechariah notes the significance of the donkey, pointing to the character of the King who was riding her, "He is humble and riding on an ass, on a colt, the offspring of a donkey." The word Zechariah uses for humble is the Hebrew word *ani*, which also means lowly, afflicted, poor, or needy. Jesus comes into Jerusalem, identifying with the poor, the lowly, the afflicted, the needy.

Luke says, "the whole throng of his disciples began rejoicing" (19:37). Who is this throng? It is not just the Twelve. It likely includes the rest of the seventy-two Jesus sent out earlier on the journey (Luke 10:1-24). It includes the women who traveled with him, supporting his work. These were the women he had healed and out of whom he had cast demons. Was the Samaritan leper there? Blind Bartimaeus? Zacchaeus? There were the tax collectors and sinners, the *'Am ha-Arez* he had loved. They were traveling with Jesus, and they were traveling to celebrate the Passover in Jerusalem. Can you picture this parade of unlikely revolutionaries? Luke tells us,

> *They praised God with a loud voice because of all the mighty things they had seen. They said,*
>
> > "Blessings on the king who comes in the name of the Lord.
> > Peace in heaven and glory in the highest heavens."
> >
> > (Luke 19:37-38)

This *is* a revolutionary scene. There is already a ruler over Jerusalem and Judea, the Roman governor Pontius Pilate. At the Temple Mount the Great Sanhedrin, comprising seventy-one leading religious authorities, were said to have "practically unlimited judicial, legislative, and administrative powers."[1] They met daily in a room at the Temple. And here was Jesus, riding a donkey down the Mount of Olives overlooking the Temple and the Holy City, his throng hailing him as the newly minted King. Jesus had already alienated the Pharisees in the Galilee and on the journey to Jerusalem. But this was a direct challenge to the authority of both Rome and the Great Sanhedrin.

This was why some of the Pharisees in the crowd that day said to Jesus, "Teacher, scold your disciples! Tell them to stop!" But Jesus replied, "I tell you, if they were silent, the stones would shout" (19:40). I think Christians often fail to see and understand the dynamics going on that day.

The Weeping King

I have walked down the Mount of Olives in Jerusalem many times. When you make this walk, you come to a small chapel, halfway down the mountain. Called the *Dominus Flevit* chapel, designed as an inverted tear, it has a magnificent view of Jerusalem and the Muslim Dome of the Rock, which sits where the Temple once stood.

When Jesus looked on Jerusalem, it caused him to weep:

> *As Jesus came to the city and observed it, he wept over it. He said, "If only you knew on this of all days the things that lead to peace. But now they are hidden from your eyes. The time will come when your enemies will build fortifications around you, encircle you, and attack you from all sides. They will crush you completely, you and the people within you. They won't leave one stone on top of another within you, because you didn't recognize the time of your gracious visit from God."*
>
> (Luke 19:41-44)

Only Luke records this. It is one of only two places in the Gospels where Jesus weeps. The other is when his friend Lazarus dies as recorded in the Gospel of John. Here Jesus predicts what will happen thirty-six years after he is crucified. He doesn't just predict it; I believe he sees it in his mind's eye. It grieves him. The Temple he called "my Father's house" in the one childhood scene we have of Jesus, in Luke 2:49, will be destroyed along with Jerusalem. But it is not just the future destruction of the Temple that grieves him. It is the slaughter of Jews he knows will happen at that time.

Dominus Flevit, a Roman Catholic church on the Mount of Olives, commemorates Jesus weeping over Jerusalem (Luke 19:37-42).

The Dome of the Rock on the site of the Temple Mount, as seen from the Dominus Flevit on the Mount of Olives.

In AD 66, some of the Jews began to protest paying taxes to Caesar. The Roman governor marched into the Temple with his soldiers and took the gold and silver from the Temple treasury, saying it was for Caesar, to make up for the taxes that were being withheld. He arrested some of the Jewish leaders as well. This act was like pouring fuel on a smoldering fire. In response, Jews revolted in Jerusalem and attacked a Roman garrison. They had some initial success. Some began to believe that this, finally, was the day God would deliver his people from foreign rule. This became known as the Great Jewish Revolt. Rome eventually sent sixty thousand troops to quell the revolt. After subduing the Galilee and Samaria, the Romans did exactly what Jesus spoke about here in Luke: they built fortifications, circled the city, attacked from all sides, and crushed the Jewish people completely. In AD 70, the Romans conquered Jerusalem and destroyed the Temple.

You'll notice that this vision of Jerusalem's future destruction is the backdrop of much of what Jesus says during Holy Week. He is challenging the religious authorities. But he also speaks of the devastation that is to come. It is interesting that Luke likely writes his Gospel in the years after the destruction of Jerusalem and the final defeat of the Jews at the hands of the Romans (the war wasn't deemed over until AD 73). Luke recounts the words of Jesus, but he does so as one who knows precisely what happened decades after Jesus was killed. He knows that tens of thousands of Jews had been taken as slaves. That under the Roman siege, Jews starved to death in Jerusalem. He knew that the Temple had been destroyed and the massive stones cast off the walls of the Temple Mount. And he knew that hundreds of thousands of Jews (first-century Jewish historian Josephus reports 1.1 million) had been killed.

No wonder Jesus weeps as he stands there looking down upon the city. As he weeps he says, "If only you knew on this of all days the things that lead to peace," and then this moving and theologically significant statement, "You didn't recognize the time of your gracious visit from God" (19:44). His coming to Jerusalem that week was the gracious visit from God that they would not recognize. There, on that mountain, the King weeps for his people.

Driving Out the Merchants and Moneychangers

Upon entering Jerusalem, Luke tells us that Jesus's first revolutionary act was not to challenge the Romans. Instead, he challenged the authority of the Sanhedrin. Luke writes, "When Jesus entered the temple, he threw out those who were selling things there. He said to them, 'It's written, *My house will be a house of prayer, but you have made it a hideout for crooks*'" (Luke 19:45-46).

Jesus and his entourage of what some would call misfits entered the Temple courts, and all must have been utterly shocked by what he did. The other Gospels give a bit more detail here. He overturns the tables of the moneychangers set up in the Temple courts and, using a whip, drives out those who were buying and selling. The Sanhedrin met in these Temple courts daily, and they sanctioned and received revenue from the merchants and moneychangers.

Why does Jesus do this? The religious authorities required that offerings be made with the Temple shekel. The Roman denarius had images of the emperor who, on the coin, was described as a "son of god." A female deity was often on the reverse side. It was seen as a graven image and idolatrous, hence not allowed to be used for offerings. So, these coins were to be exchanged for coins that could be offered, the Temple shekel. But the moneychangers charged a premium for these coins. This had a particular impact upon the poor.

Likewise, the religious authorities made clear that only animals of a certain quality could be sacrificed in the Temple. It was far better to purchase your offering, a certified animal, in the Temple courts than to risk bringing your own animal for sacrifice and having it rejected. These "certified" animals also came with a premium price.

Once more, the common people were being taken advantage of by the merchants, who were giving a portion of their take to the religious authorities.

It is no wonder that Jesus was angry. God's people were being taken advantage of when they were coming to make their required offerings to God. And the response of the religious leaders at the Temple was precisely what Jesus expected: "The chief priests, the legal experts, and the foremost leaders among the people were seeking to kill him" (Luke 19:47). Once again, Jesus spoke up on behalf of the lowly, and this act sealed his fate.

> ## Jesus spoke up on behalf of the lowly, and this act sealed his fate.

As you read Luke 21, you'll see the religious leaders, the highest authority in first-century Judaism, questioning Jesus about *his* authority. From Luke's perspective, knowing that in Jesus God had come to earth, it is an absurd line of questioning pointing to the blindness of these authorities. They continue to try to trap Jesus with questions that will turn either the crowd or the Romans against him. In turn, Jesus tells parables that are veiled references to the religious authorities. The crowds, particularly the *'Am ha-Arez* and others who had felt judged by the religious authorities, hung on Jesus's every word so that the religious authorities found themselves hesitant to act on their desire to arrest Jesus because they were afraid of the crowds.

Give to Caesar, Give to God

One of the questions the religious leaders posed to Jesus as the crowd listened, a question designed to trap him, was, "Does the Law allow people to pay taxes to Caesar or not?" (Luke 20:22).

The seeds of the later revolt of AD 66, which started over paying taxes to Rome, were present in Jesus's day as well. When the religious leaders asked Jesus for his thoughts on paying taxes, they felt they had him trapped. The people who followed Jesus disliked paying taxes. If Jesus answered yes, it is lawful to pay taxes to Caesar, he would lose the favor of the crowd. If he said no, he would be arrested for revolting against Rome.

Jesus avoids the trap with a response that is both clever and insightful.

> "Show me a coin. Whose image and inscription does it have on it?"

> "Caesar's," they replied.

> He said to them, "Give to Caesar what belongs to Caesar and to God what belongs to God."

(Luke 20:24-25)

Genesis says that we were created in the "image of God." The Roman coin had an image of the emperor. Humans are created in the image of God. Give to Caesar what bears his image [the coin with which taxes are paid] and to give to God what bears God's image [your lives!].

The Widow's Mite

Jesus taught again about money when he saw people making donations to the Temple treasury.

> Looking up, Jesus saw rich people throwing their gifts into the collection box for the temple treasury. He also saw a poor widow throw in two small copper coins worth a penny. He said, "I assure you that this poor widow has put in more than them all. All of them are giving out of their spare change. But she from her hopeless poverty has given everything she had to live on."

(Luke 21:1-4)

This passage has been interpreted in different ways. Some read this story as though Jesus is pointing to the woman as an example of the religious leaders taking advantage of poor widows. In the verse just before this story, Luke 20:47, Jesus condemned the religious leaders who "cheat widows out of their homes." Just after saying this, Jesus looks up to see a widow giving her last two small coins—the widow's mite. This appears to be the very thing that Jesus has condemned about the religious leaders.

While this may have been part of his point, I think his primary aim was to honor the poor widow and her faith. Most people would have paid little attention to the elderly widow putting in her tiny coins. It might have seemed an insignificant amount to them, particularly when there were wealthy people sometimes making a big deal about stuffing large numbers of coins into the receptacles used for the offering. But, Jesus said, that's not how God sees this woman. God sees her gift as the great sacrifice that it is. Jesus recognizes that what she gives is a large amount to her, and he sees that her offering is more than that of all the people tossing in their bags of silver and gold.

Jesus didn't diminish the offerings the others gave that day, but he was pointing out a principle of God's economics. Some might give dramatically more in the offering, yet God recognizes that it was the *relative sacrifice* that mattered. She gave far more in her offering than these who, out of their excess, gave to God.

Once more, in this story, we see Jesus lifting up the lowly, and telling us that God doesn't see the number of zeroes in our giving, but the relative sacrifice we're making when we give. Organizations tend to name buildings after major donors, but often the more sacrificial gifts come from people whose names will never be on a building.

The Destruction of the Temple

We learned earlier that Luke likely wrote his Gospel in the years following the Roman destruction of Jerusalem and its Temple. Luke's recounting of Jesus's words, given nearly forty years earlier, are both tragic and enigmatic. Christians have been debating the meaning of these words ever since.

Jesus appears to be saying that he will return for the Last Judgment soon after the destruction of Jerusalem. The early church certainly believed that Christ's return was imminent. In Luke 21, after describing the Roman devastation of Jerusalem, he records these words of Jesus: "Then they will see 'the Son of Man coming in a cloud' with power and great glory. Now when these things begin to take place, stand up and raise your heads, because your redemption is drawing near" (Luke 21:27-28 NRSV).

There have been multiple different ways interpreters have tried to understand these passages in the Gospels. I'll encourage you to explore these various views on your own. When I read Revelation, or these apocalyptic passages in the Gospels, it strikes me that every generation or century has seen similar events that occur—not the destruction of the Temple, but wars and rumors of wars, earthquakes and famines, and the seeming triumph of evil. There are false messiahs and antichrists that have appeared throughout history.

Perhaps Jesus's words were meant to say that none of these things will have the final word. Darkness will, in the end, be defeated by light over and over again. I think of Dr. King's words, "The arc of the moral universe is long, but it bends toward justice."[2] At hundreds of times throughout history people must have felt the end was upon them. I think of World War II, Hitler, and the Holocaust as a time in which the events of Revelation and the small apocalypses, as they are called, in the Gospels, clearly could be seen in the events taking place in Europe. Yet darkness was ultimately defeated.

Jesus's words in Luke 21:34-36 (NRSV) seem important:

> *"Be on guard so that your hearts are not weighed down with dissipation and drunkenness and the worries of this life, and that day does not catch you unexpectedly, like a trap. For it will come upon all who live on the face of the whole earth. Be alert at all times, praying that you*

may have the strength to escape all these things that will take place, and to stand before the Son of Man."

In the end, Christ will return. Until then, we trust in him, we pay attention, and we work to push back the darkness. We live as people who are ready to meet Christ face to face. We are meant to be, as Zechariah once wrote, "prisoners of hope," knowing that the present darkness, whatever it may be, will not ultimately prevail.

The Last Supper:
Who Is the Greatest

This takes us to Thursday, the day of the Last Supper, the Passover meal. By way of this meal, the Jewish people remembered that they once had been slaves in Egypt, but God had delivered them. At the meal, Jesus and his disciples would recount the events of the Passover and God's deliverance.

Jesus sent two of his disciples to prepare the meal earlier in the day. The disciples would gather in an upper room belonging to someone who sympathized with Jesus. That night during the meal, Jesus said, "I have earnestly desired to eat this Passover with you before I suffer" (Luke 22:15). That set the tone for the dinner. Jesus reinterpreted the meal that night. He was the lamb to be slaughtered to rescue his people from death. The unleavened bread was his body. The cup was his blood initiating a new covenant. He was freeing his people from slavery to sin and death.

The New Testament gives us the basic outline of the meal, but Jesus doesn't fully explain it. Christians continued to reflect upon this meal long after Jesus's death and resurrection. Just as Jesus routinely broke bread with people, befriending them and making them his companions (*com paneri*—breaking bread with), he does that with us as we share in this meal. In this holy meal we remember what God has done for us in Jesus. We remember his life, his death, and his resurrection. We recall his love and his grace for sinners like us. We eat and drink and in so doing, we partake of him, his body and blood given for us and our sins. We meet him in the breaking of the bread. And we remember that he promised we would eat this meal again with him in the kingdom of heaven.

That night, as Jesus sat at the table, he had to have looked around at his disciples and wondered if the movement he began would continue after he was gone. Sitting next to him was Judas. Jesus knew that Judas had already sold him out for silver and would lead a group of soldiers to arrest Jesus later that night. He knew that Simon Peter would deny knowing him three times. He knew that the other ten disciples would all flee in the darkness after he was taken away. Yet he shared this meal with them.

Jesus knows this of us when we come to the table. He knows that we both long to follow him, and we struggle at times to be faithful. He knows that we love him and sometimes betray him. He knows that we have pledged to "go with him, with him all the way" but when things get hard, we might just deny knowing him. Yet he still invites us to his table, eager to break bread with us and to offer us forgiveness once again. From the meal, through his crucifixion and resurrection, the disciples will struggle to understand.

That night of all nights, after the supper was over, "an argument broke out among the disciples over which one of them should be regarded as the greatest" (Luke 22:24).

Jesus is about to give his life for his people, but the disciples don't understand. Instead, they are arguing over which of them was the greatest. This is the second time in Luke that they are having this argument (the other is Luke 9:46). This time, Jesus responds by teaching them what it means to be the greatest in God's kingdom.

Jesus said to them, "The kings of the Gentiles rule over their subjects, and those in authority over them are called 'friends of the people.' But that's not the way it will be with you. Instead, the greatest among you must become like a person of lower status and the leader like a servant."

(Luke 22:25-26)

On the last night of his life, at his last supper, Jesus puts into words what we've seen throughout the entire Gospel. This is what he's done in befriending outsiders and outcasts, in seeking to lift up the lowly. He came as a servant-king. Everything we've seen to this point in the Gospel is a picture of Jesus doing what finally now he puts into words. He gave himself to love, heal, and care for the broken and hurting. He sought to show mercy and grace to the marginalized and those far from God. He came to see those who were often overlooked or unseen. And if he did that for us, as his disciples this must be our posture and the mission we are called to as well. This is what it means to be his disciple: we follow him, and we lift up the lowly.

Lifting up the lowly requires becoming lowly. Greatness is defined by lowering ourselves and serving others. In our world, this is utterly countercultural, but it is absolutely the culture of the Kingdom.

If the disciples, who spent three years with Jesus, were still focused on status and power at the Last Supper, it should not surprise us that we struggle with these same things at times as well. But nearly every one of the conversations Jesus had over his final week were on this same theme. He encouraged a rich young ruler to lay down the source of his status. He blessed and healed a blind beggar. He befriended a wealthy and powerful tax collector who gave up half of what he had to the poor. He praised the poor widow while castigating the powerful and status-loving religious elite. "The greatest among you must become like a person of lower status and the leader like a servant" (Luke 22:6).

6

CRUCIFIED WITH THE OUTLAWS

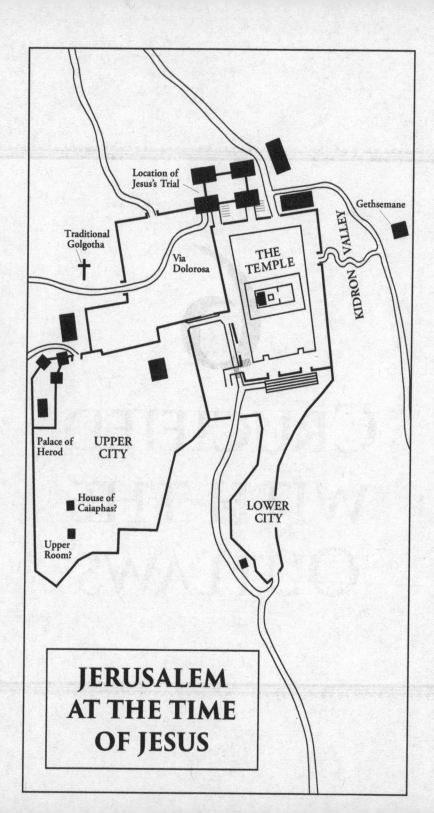

Location of Jesus's Trial

Traditional Golgotha

Via Dolorosa

THE TEMPLE

Gethsemane

KIDRON VALLEY

Palace of Herod

UPPER CITY

House of Caiaphas?

Upper Room?

LOWER CITY

JERUSALEM AT THE TIME OF JESUS

6

CRUCIFIED WITH THE OUTLAWS

They also led two other criminals to be executed with Jesus. When they arrived at the place called Skull, they crucified him, along with the criminals, one on his right and the other on his left. Jesus said, "Father, forgive them, for they don't know what they're doing." . . .

One of the criminals hanging next to Jesus insulted him: "Aren't you the Christ? Save yourself and us!"

Responding, the other criminal spoke harshly to him, "Don't you fear God, seeing that you've also been sentenced to die? We are rightly condemned, for we are receiving the appropriate sentence for what we did. But this man has done nothing wrong." Then he said, "Jesus, remember me when you come into your kingdom."

Jesus replied, "I assure you that today you will be with me in paradise."

(Luke 23:32-43)

Throughout this book, I've not attempted a verse-by-verse commentary on Luke. Instead, I've hoped to help you see what I believe is the major premise of Luke's Gospel: Jesus's concern for the outsiders, outcasts, and outlaws—the *'Am ha-Arez*. Contrary to the way many of these people were made to feel by some among the religious leadership in first-century Judaism, Jesus conveyed a clear sense of God's love and mercy for them and focused on calling them to return to God. In Luke 5:32, Jesus captured this by saying, "I didn't come to call righteous people but sinners to change their hearts and lives." His driving passion for those who were considered sinners and lost sheep is clear in Luke 19:10, as we saw in the previous chapter, "The Son of Man came to seek and to save the lost" (NRSV).

Up to this point, Luke has focused primarily on Jesus's concern for the outsiders and outcasts. But when we come to the Crucifixion, Luke highlights Jesus's concern for the outlaws, even as Jesus himself is put on trial, convicted, and counted among the criminals.

After the Supper

After the supper was over and Jesus had reminded his disciples that greatness is defined by serving, Jesus sought to prepare his disciples for his arrest later that night. He urged them, "Take your wallet or your bag, and if you don't have a sword, sell your clothes to buy one." He was preparing them for the fact they soon might be fleeing and needing both money and some means of protecting themselves. Why would they need this? Because, Jesus said, "I tell you that this scripture must be fulfilled in relation to me: And *he was counted among criminals*. Indeed, what's written about me is nearing completion" (Luke 22:37). Jesus was about to be arrested, tried, convicted, beaten, and sentenced to die an outlaw's death.

Jesus spoke these words just before leading the disciples to Gethsemane. Did Jesus literally want them to sell their clothing that night and buy swords as they went? It was late into the night and that seems unlikely. And why would the man who taught them to love their enemy and to turn the other cheek ask them to buy swords?

Interpreters agree on one thing and disagree on another. They agree that Jesus was trying to say, "Pay attention, things are about to get bad. I'll be counted among the outlaws, and by extension, as my followers, you will be too. Earlier in our ministry, I told you not to take a purse and to trust that God would take care of you. Now

I'm telling you, take your wallets and your bags, and even have a sword, because things are about to get very difficult."

Where there is some disagreement is if Jesus really intended them to carry swords and to be prepared to fight. It's an interesting passage in a world where there is a great deal of debate about weapons and violence. Some read the passage and say, "Look, even Jesus says that his disciples should be 'packing' so they can protect themselves!" Others say, "Jesus didn't intend for them to use swords, he was speaking in hyperbole once again to make a point." The interpreters in this latter category note that the disciples took Jesus literally and said, "Jesus, look, we've already got two swords!" To which Jesus replied, "Enough of that!" as if frustrated that the disciples did not get the point. A short time later, in Gethsemane, one of the disciples pulls a sword and strikes the high priest's servant's ear. Jesus responded, "Stop! No more of this!" These would argue that the man who said "Love your enemy" and "Turn the other cheek" would not have asked his disciples to use swords to defend themselves.

Here's the key thing to notice from this story in Luke 22:35-38, a story that appears nowhere else in the Gospels: Jesus is about to be considered a criminal, an outlaw, and, by extension, the disciples would be branded outlaws as well.

Praying on the Mount of Olives

After this warning, Jesus leads his disciples out of the guest room where they had shared the meal. They had spent each night since coming to Jerusalem on the Mount of Olives, and they would return there one final time. The walk from the traditional site of the upper room to the traditional site of Gethsemane is about twenty minutes. They descended into the Kidron Valley. To their left was the Temple, to their right the tombs of princes, priests, and powerful people, some of which are still standing today.

Luke simply tells us that Jesus and the disciples made their way to the Mount of Olives. Matthew and Mark tell us that Jesus led them to "a place called Gethsemane." John tells us that Jesus led them to a garden on the Mount of Olives. Bringing the readings together, we have the garden of Gethsemane. The location is usually identified with a grove of olive trees, some very old, at the base of the Mount of Olives where the Basilica of Christ's Agony, also known as the Church of All Nations, stands. The trees are just outside the church. The church is among my favorite in the Holy Land as it is intended, as you enter the church, to transport you to the night of Christ's agony. Tile mosaics of trees ascend the columns with the branches covering parts of the ceiling. It is night and the stars are seen overhead. As you enter the church, you enter the garden with the disciples. Straight ahead, above the altar, is a mosaic of Jesus praying in agony, leaning against a rock formation. Below this mosaic, in front of the altar, is an actual rock formation where one can imagine Jesus praying. Worshippers kneel at the rock formation and touch it as they pray, perhaps joining Jesus in this prayer, "Not my will, but thy will be done."

At the same time, perhaps a more likely site for Gethsemane is a short walk from the church and olive grove. There is a cave called the Grotto of Gethsemane. It is thought to have housed an ancient olive oil press, and the name, Gethsemane, means oil press in Aramaic. Christians visited this site from at least the 300s if not earlier, seeing the grotto as the place Jesus and the disciples slept on the Mount of Olives and hence the likely location of Jesus's arrest.

Whether Jesus prayed in the grotto, among the trees, or somewhere near this rock formation makes little difference. Each of these places brings the story to life in a powerful way.

Upon arriving at the Mount of Olives, Jesus says to his disciples:

"Pray that you won't give in to temptation." He withdrew from them about a stone's throw, knelt down, and prayed. He said, "Father, if it's

your will, take this cup of suffering away from me. However, not my will but your will must be done."

(Luke 22:40-42)

Christians throughout the ages have found in Jesus's prayer at Gethsemane a model or pattern of prayer for their lives and a source of comfort and guidance for Christians enduring suffering. Though Jesus has been predicting his death since Luke 9 and he believes his death will be redemptive, he still asks for God to "take this cup of suffering away from me." We see Jesus's humanity in this prayer. He doesn't want to suffer, prays not to suffer, but in the end is willing to suffer if his suffering is essential for God's redemptive purposes.

> Suffering is not God's plan, nor does it happen at God's initiative.... But when these things do happen, God acts both to strengthen us and, ultimately, to redeem our suffering.

For most of us, suffering is not God's plan, nor does it happen at God's initiative—God does not give us cancer, or place it on the hearts of others to commit acts of violence or injustice against us, to wage wars, to lie or cheat or steal or to otherwise inflict pain upon us. Scripture makes clear that these are typically not God's will. But when these things do happen, God acts both to strengthen us and, ultimately, to redeem our suffering. The violence against Jesus will be the initiative of those who taunt, torture, and kill him. But God knew these things would happen and planned to use them as instruments of redemption.

115

An Angel and Perspiring Blood

The details we read in Luke 22:43-44 only appear in Luke's Gospel, and then only in some early copies of Luke, but not in others. The verses read:

Then a heavenly angel appeared to him and strengthened him. He was in anguish and prayed even more earnestly. His sweat became like drops of blood falling down on the ground.

(Luke 22:43-44)

This is a passage about which there has been great debate as to whether it was originally part of Luke's Gospel. Remember, we don't have any of the original documents of the New Testament. Why not? For several reasons including the fact that the original manuscripts were very quickly copied and circulated to others who would be interested in reading a Gospel, or a letter from Paul or another apostle. The first-century Christians may have had little thought that they should preserve the original once there were plenty of copies in circulation. This seems important to us, nearly two millennia later, but not to them. In addition, in the ancient world, manuscripts were typically handwritten on parchment (animal skins) or papyrus (paper made from strips of the papyrus plant). Over time and with frequent use these could fade, or become brittle, or otherwise become illegible. When that happened they would be retired or discarded, replaced by new versions.

The earliest fragments of New Testament documents date back to the 100s, and only a few of these exist. More exist from the 200s, and more still from the 300s and 400s. Altogether, some five thousand-plus manuscripts of New Testament documents date back to the year 1000 or before. As these documents were copied, there were occasional changes that happened to the text. Generally, the New Testament documents evidence a very careful and accurate transmission. But sometimes different or variant readings crept into the process. Scribes might make an error. Sometimes they would include lines seeking to clarify or correct something in the version that had been passed down to them. There were some additions or deletions from a few Gospel stories. These variant versions were then passed down and recopied. So modern scholars, called "textual critics," have made it their life's work to look over all the ancient manuscripts, attempting to discern which of the variants of the ancient New Testament manuscripts reflect the earliest and closest reading to what the New Testament authors originally wrote. The case is similar for the writings of the Old Testament.

Which takes us back to Luke 22:43-44. Many of the earliest copies of Luke's Gospel do not contain these verses. Others do contain them. And some of the second-century Christian writings refer to these verses. The question then has been hotly debated among scholars whether these two verses were originally in Luke or not. Some have argued that they were not and were added later to show God's provision for Jesus in the garden (the angel) and the intensity of Jesus's anguish (the sweat mingled with blood). Others believe these were originally a part of Luke's Gospel but made some early scribes uncomfortable because they made Jesus out to be far too human, in fear and anguish before his arrest. By removing these two verses they were toning down Luke's portrayal of a very human Jesus. Take a look in your own Bible at these verses and see if they are in brackets, as in the NRSV, or have a footnote, as in the NIV, or are simply included with no note, as in the CEB, or not included at all, as in the RSV.

However these verses came to us, I am grateful they are included in most of our Bibles. In these verses we see that Jesus is not a machine; he is a human being. Divine, yes, but also, as the Chalcedonian Creed makes clear, "truly human." Jesus experiences anguish and fear. Matthew and Mark make this point as well. But by the time John was written, John seems almost embarrassed to show

Jesus's humanity in such an intense way. John's account of Jesus's arrest in the garden doesn't mention his anguish at all. Instead, when the soldiers come to arrest Jesus, they fall back in fear when Jesus identifies himself.

Luke 22:43-44 makes clear that Jesus struggled, was afraid, and experienced anxiety and anguish. Jesus's response to this fear and anxiety was to pray. And as he prayed, an angel came to strengthen him. The angel did not rescue him from this situation and save Jesus from the cross. The angel strengthened him for the journey ahead. What are we to make of Luke noting that Jesus perspired drops of blood? Again, no other gospel tells us this. The perspiring of drops of blood is a known, but rare medical condition called *hematidrosis*. It is thought to be caused by intense anxiety when our body's fight-or-flight mechanism narrows the capillaries to prepare us for actions in the face of fear. If the fear is suddenly relieved, the capillaries dilate and, in some cases, rupture, leaving blood entering the sweat glands. It might actually be a sign of a very rapid relief from anxiety.[1]

This response would line up with an angel strengthening Jesus in the midst of his intense fear. The drops of sweat comingled with blood thus testifies both to the anguish and fear of Jesus, and the release he had as he prayed and found God's help through the messenger God sent (the Greek word for *angel* means "messenger").

This also points to a theme we've not touched on, namely that in Luke's Gospel Jesus prays, and prays a lot. In 3:21-22, it is while he is praying as he is baptized that the Holy Spirit comes upon him and he hears the voice of his Father saying, "You are my Son, whom I dearly love; in you I find happiness." In 5:16, Luke writes, "Jesus would withdraw to deserted places for prayer." In 6:12, Jesus prays to God "all night long" before choosing his twelve disciples. In Luke 9:18, he prays by himself. In Luke 9:28, he takes Peter, John, and James up on a mountain to pray, and while he prays he is radiantly transformed. In 11:1, as Jesus was praying, his disciples noticed and asked him to teach them to pray, and he taught them to pray the Lord's Prayer. There are other times Jesus prays, but in Gethsemane, we see Jesus modeling for us the practice of praying when in anguish and filled with anxiety. The prayer doesn't remove the threat, but it does provide strength for Jesus in the midst of despair.

Slicing Off, and Healing, a Slave's Ear

In verse 45, Jesus returns to the disciples and finds them asleep. Luke downplays this story compared with Matthew and Mark, and John leaves the story out altogether. Yet even in Luke Jesus finds his disciples have fallen asleep as he prayed. By this time, the disciples are grieving too, though they still don't fully understand what is about to happen.

Just then, as in all of the Gospels, Judas Iscariot, one of Jesus's disciples, shows up leading a crowd to arrest Jesus. As Jesus and the Twelve are surrounded by these soldiers, one of the disciples (in John's Gospel, we learn it was Simon Peter) pulls out a sword and slices off the ear of a slave, the slave of the high priest who is seeking to kill Jesus. Notice how Jesus responded: "Stop! No more of this!" (Luke 22:51). He then touched the slave's ear and healed him.

Don't miss this: Jesus is about to be arrested, then put to death. He has been in intense anguish. The sweat mixed with blood is still on his brow, yet he stops to heal the slave of the man who wants him put to death. Even here, in this moment of agony, Jesus is focused on lifting up the lowly. While all the Gospels describe the man's ear being cut off, only Luke tells us that Jesus bent down to pick up the man's ear and to heal him. Once more, I am moved by Jesus and his compassion for the lowly.

The Denial

Jesus is arrested, though Luke doesn't tell us precisely what happened to the disciples at that moment. Presumably most of them fled. But Peter does what he promised he would do: he follows at a distance, going with Jesus to the trial before the Jewish Sanhedrin—the religious authorities.

What follows is the story of Peter's denial of Jesus. All four Gospels record that Jesus was taken to the high priest's home for trial. Luke, like the others, has Peter denying he was a disciple of Jesus or even knew him. Three times this happens. In Luke, after the third denial, we read:

> At that very moment, while he was still speaking, a rooster crowed. The Lord turned and looked straight at Peter, and Peter remembered the Lord's words: "Before a rooster crows today, you will deny me three times." And Peter went out and cried uncontrollably.
>
> (Luke 22:60b-62)

It has always been interesting to me that all four Gospels include this story of Peter's denial of Jesus. This was the most ignominious moment of his life. Why would they tell this story? Each of the Gospels was written after Peter's death. It seems particularly surprising that they would tell this story about a man who would go on to be one of the heroes of the faith. Generally, after the death of someone who was highly revered, we don't tell stories of their greatest failures. Which leads me to this thought: perhaps the reason they were comfortable telling this story is because Peter himself told this story as a part of his witness everywhere he preached in the years after Jesus's death. It was so well known that even John, which often differs from Matthew, Mark, and Luke, is compelled to include it. And why would Peter tell this story wherever he preached? Perhaps he knew that we all have moments when, by our words and actions, we deny Jesus.

I find as a pastor my people appreciate me the most when I share with them my shortcomings and failures. It means I'm human. And, if I as their pastor fail, there is hope for them if they fail. Peter's denial and subsequent restoration by Jesus gave hope for all Christians who heard this story. That, I think, is why the Gospels repeatedly tell this story. If Peter succumbed to fear and his courage failed him, yet Jesus took him back, will he not do the same for us? I'm always moved by the last line in this part of the story: "And Peter went out and cried uncontrollably." Can you think of a time, or times, when you have denied Jesus? I can think of many. And I'm grateful he takes us back.

> # If Peter succumbed to fear and his courage failed him, yet Jesus took him back, will he not do the same for us?

The Trials

During Peter's ordeal in the courtyard, Jesus is awaiting trial inside the house. Unlike Matthew and Mark where Jesus's trial before the Sanhedrin begins at night, Luke tells us only that, "the men who were holding Jesus in custody taunted him while they beat him. They blindfolded him and asked him repeatedly, 'Prophesy! Who hit you?' Insulting him, they said many other horrible things against him" (Luke 22:63-65).

In the morning, Luke tells us, the Sanhedrin gather and bring Jesus before them for his first trial. Luke's account is much abbreviated but draws upon Mark and Matthew's accounts. The Sanhedrin then takes Jesus to Pontius Pilate, twisting his words (in the case of paying taxes, they accuse him of saying the opposite of what he actually had taught). But they correctly note that Jesus claimed that "he is the Christ, a king." Jesus had done this not in so many words, but by riding the donkey into Jerusalem, intentionally fulfilling Zechariah's words.

Luke's description of the trial before Pilate is likewise brief. Pilate finds no "legal basis for action against this man." Luke continues with the accusations against Jesus, noting, "They [the chief priests and the crowds] objected strenuously, saying, 'He agitates the people with his teaching throughout Judea—starting from Galilee all the way here'" (Luke 23:5). *Agitate* here implies seeking to move the people to rebellion. But Jesus wasn't agitating them to rebel against Rome. He was agitating the people, if that word could describe his ministry, to rebel against a religious hypocrisy of rules that made the ordinary people, the *'Am ha-Arez*, second class and estranged from God. He was agitating the crowds by calling out this hypocrisy and showing them that they were valued by God, sought after by God, and loved by God.

Pilate, upon learning that Jesus was from the Galilee, and knowing that Herod Antipas, the ruler of the Galilee, is in Jerusalem for the Passover, sends Jesus for a third trial, to stand before Herod. This is the same Herod who had John the Baptist put to death. Luke notes, "Herod was very glad to see Jesus, for he had heard about Jesus and had wanted to see him for quite some time. He was hoping to see Jesus perform some sign" (Luke 23:8). Herod questions Jesus, but Jesus remains silent. I wonder what Jesus must have felt being questioned by the man who had executed his friend and cousin, John—a man whom John had publicly criticized for his immorality. Once more, the religious authorities standing before Herod accuse Jesus of crimes. Jesus refuses to speak to Herod, and Herod and his soldiers, in turn, treat Jesus with contempt. It is here that Jesus is mocked as Herod places a royal robe upon Jesus, as if he were a king, then sends him back to Pilate. This trial is not mentioned in any of the other Gospels, but it is fascinating.

Then Pilate called together the chief priests, the rulers, and the people. He said to them, "You brought this man before me as one who was misleading the people. I have questioned him in your presence and found nothing in this man's conduct that provides a legal basis for the charges you have brought against him. Neither did Herod, because Herod returned him to us. He's done nothing that deserves death. Therefore, I'll have him whipped, then let him go."

(Luke 23:13-16)

Jesus has been tried before the religious leaders, but Pilate now includes "the people." Which people? Luke does not say, but it is not all the people, and it seems likely that some in this crowd are the merchants and moneychangers whose tables Jesus overturned when he first entered Jerusalem. Jesus is thus four times strenuously accused of being an outlaw by the religious leaders.

Pilate will have Jesus whipped, hoping it will appease the crowd. But they are not appeased. The earliest manuscripts of Luke do not have Luke 23:17, "*He had to release one prisoner for them because of the festival.*" This was likely added later, drawn from Matthew and Mark's accounts of the trial. In either case, the crowd of religious leaders, Temple merchants, and others begin to shout, "'Away with this man! Release Barabbas to us.' (Barabbas had been thrown into prison because of a riot that had occurred in the city, and for murder.)" (23:18b-19).

Once more, in verse 22, Luke notes, "For the third time, Pilate said to them, 'Why? What wrong has he done? I've found no legal basis for the death penalty in his case. Therefore, I will have him whipped, then let him go.'" Three times the Roman legate pronounce Jesus's innocence. Six times the religious authorities pronounce him guilty and worthy of death. They go so far as to demand that Pilate release an actual murderer and insurgent while putting Jesus, the man who calls for his followers to love their enemies, to death. Luke tells us:

They were adamant, shouting their demand that Jesus be crucified. Their voices won out. Pilate issued his decision to grant their request. He released the one they asked for, who had been thrown into prison because of a riot and murder. But he handed Jesus over to their will.

(Luke 23:23-25)

123

Jesus was, as he had foretold, "counted among criminals" (22:37). And Jesus's sentence to die, while Barabbas is set free, is a foreshadowing of the idea that Jesus's death was *for us*, that we might be set free.

Crucified

Crucifixions happened outside the city walls. A tall vertical beam, called the *stipes*, was thought to have been kept at the site of crucifixions, a place called *Golgotha* in Aramaic, *Kranion* in Greek, and *Calvary* in Latin—the Place of the Skull. The crossbeam, called the *patibulum*, was often carried to the site by those sentenced to die.

Unlike John, who portrays Jesus as strong enough to carry his cross, Luke tells us that Simon of Cyrene, a city on the coast of North Africa, is pressed into service to carry the cross. Luke notes that among the "huge crowd" of people following Jesus to the place of crucifixion were "women who were mourning and wailing" (23:27), likely the same women who had been following Jesus and supporting his ministry. Not surprisingly, it is only Luke among the four Gospel writers who tells us about these women following Jesus to the cross and the conversation Jesus has with them as he prepares for his execution.

There were two other criminals taken to be crucified with Jesus. Once at Calvary, their crosses were assembled, the victims were stripped naked, and they were nailed to their cross. Then the crosses were hoisted into the air. These crosses, from the little evidence we have, were not terribly tall. Those crucified were only a few feet off the ground, quite different from the usual portrayal of the cross in classic art.

Jesus hung between two criminals, literally counted among the criminals, dying the death of an outlaw. The Gospels record that Jesus spoke seven times from the cross during those six hours that he hung dying, from 9 a.m. to 3 p.m.[2] These statements are often referred to as "the Seven Last Words of Jesus." By way of reminder, these are the last words or statements of Jesus in Matthew, Mark, and John:

- "My God, my God, why have you forsaken me?" (Matthew and Mark)
- To Mary: "Woman, here is your son." To John, "Here is your mother." (John)
- "I am thirsty." (John)
- "It is finished." (John)

Let's consider the final words of Jesus in Luke's Gospel.

Father, Forgive Them...

As Jesus hangs on the cross, the soldiers mock him and gamble for his clothing. The leaders and people jeer at him. Even one of the criminals crucified beside him insults him. In the context of the blood, the pain, the cruelty and inhumanity, Jesus prays, "Father, forgive them, for they don't know what they're doing" (Luke 23:24).

Can you imagine that? He is praying for the people who are killing him. The "them" he prays for his Father to forgive includes the religious leaders, the Roman soldiers, and the criminals hanging nearby. It also includes his disciples who deserted him and Peter who denied him. Might it have also included Judas who betrayed him?

Do you know who else the "them" includes that Jesus prays for his Father to forgive? It includes you and me. We were a part of that "them." Some early Christians saw Jesus as a high priest, offering an atoning sacrifice to make amends for the sins of the world. And he himself was the sacrifice. As he suffers and dies, he pleads with God his Father on our behalf.

According to the Mishnah, the written version of Israel's oral laws, when someone was executed, they were to pray, "May my death atone for all of my sins." Here, Jesus had no sins to atone for, but he

125

does see his death as an atonement—not for his sins, but for ours. In essence he says, *not* "May my death atone for all of *my* sins," but "May my death atone for all of *their* sins."

When we look at the cross, we see the mercy and love of God for sinners and Christ's willingness to forgive.

When we look at the cross, we see the mercy and love of God for sinners and Christ's willingness to forgive. Paul writes in Romans 5:6-8, twenty years before Luke wrote his Gospel, "While we were still weak, at the right moment, Christ died for ungodly people. It isn't often that someone will die for a righteous person, though maybe someone might dare to die for a good person. But God shows his love for us, because while we were still sinners Christ died for us." His death was for us.

I meet people who feel that their sins are unforgivable, or who carry a load of guilt with them. Guilt can be good when it leads us to repentance. But at some point, after we repent, guilt becomes a burden. When we accept these words of Jesus from the cross and the forgiveness they convey, it lifts up this burden from us and sets us free from our guilt.

Not long ago a story made news out of Rochester, New York. It was the trial of a young man named Justin Seabon. A year before, he had been driving, in broad daylight, while intoxicated. He came around a corner and ran into a car in which eighty-three-year-old Milton Harris was sitting. Harris was a kind and caring man who, until the day he died, was still cutting yards for his neighbors. As Seabon's car struck Harris's car, the older man was killed instantly. At Seabon's trial, Harris's children were there. Seabon pleaded guilty, and as he entered his plea, through tears, he repeatedly said to the family, "I am so sorry. I am so sorry. I am so sorry." Milton Harris's daughter, Carol Hannah, walked over to Justin Seabon and took the man responsible for her father's death in her arms, held him for over a minute, and told him she forgave him.[3]

Seabon found deliverance in that hug, but so did Carol Hannah, as the anger and resentment began to give way to mercy. Carol's act of forgiveness lifted both of them up, him from guilt, her from bitterness. Where did they learn that this, not vengeance, was the way? We all stand in need of saving grace. One important theory of the atonement sees Christ's death on the cross as God's way of saying, "I've borne your sin, I've paid your debt." Jesus still prays that prayer for you: "Father, forgive him, forgive her, forgive them, for they don't know what they're doing."

Today You Will Be with Me in Paradise

Luke alone records a conversation that happened between Jesus and the criminals on their crosses. Luke calls the two men crucified with Jesus *kakourgai*—from the Greek words *kaka*, which means evil or bad, and *ourgai*, which are works. These are men who did evil deeds. Matthew and Mark call them something else: *lestai*, which often signifies armed and violent bandits—armed thieves willing to commit violent acts to take what they wanted. They were often seen as terrorists as they enjoyed making Romans their victims.

According to Luke, one of the criminals speaks up, insulting Jesus, mocking him from his cross. "Aren't you the Christ? Save yourself and us!" he says to Jesus (Luke 23:39). Even a guy being crucified wants to feel superior to another man on a cross. He, and the crowd around Jesus, are dehumanizing him. It wasn't enough to torture him to death. They lost all compassion and humanity. But that wasn't true of the other criminal who hung the other side of Jesus.

127

That man spoke up, saying to the first criminal, "Don't you fear God, seeing that you've also been sentenced to die? We are rightly condemned, for we are receiving the appropriate sentence for what we did. But this man has done nothing wrong." And then he turns to Jesus saying, "Jesus, remember me when you come into your kingdom" (Luke 23:40-42).

One way of reading the Gospels is to put yourself in the story. Here are two criminals who share the same fate as Jesus. One is kind, the other cruel. We're meant to see ourselves as one of these thieves. We might be the angry thief who insists on insulting Jesus as if, even as he is dying, he takes delight in supposing that there is still one person of lower status than he. But we might also identify with the thief on the cross who speaks up for Jesus, then calls upon Jesus, praying that Jesus will remember him when he comes into his kingdom. Like the tax collector in a parable we considered earlier in this book, who prayed, "God, show mercy to me, a sinner," the thief on the cross next to Jesus models a prayer for us as he says, "Jesus, remember me when you come into your kingdom." This is a powerful prayer and one you might find compelling to incorporate into your prayer life. As you ask Jesus to remember you, recall that in scripture, when God is said to remember someone, he inevitably acts on the person's behalf.

Jesus responds to the man, "I assure you that today you will be with me in paradise" (Luke 23:43). In first-century Judaism, Hades or Sheol was the realm of the dead. Within that realm, there was a place of suffering for the unrighteous dead called Gehenna. And there was a place for the righteous dead called Paradise.

On this day, Jesus assured this criminal that he would be with Jesus in the realm of the righteous dead, not because of anything this man had done, except to identify with Jesus and to ask for his grace. It is a compelling picture that salvation and grace are a gift, not based upon anything we had done apart from identifying with Jesus and asking him to rescue us.

I love this passage, found only in Luke, because here we see, to the very end, even as he hung dying on the cross, Jesus is seeking to rescue or save the lost. And while the criminal couldn't do anything to atone for his sin, he trusted in Jesus. Jesus offered him grace and promised to welcome him to paradise.

Darkness Covered the Land

After Jesus speaks to the criminal on the cross, Luke recounts the details of Jesus's death. "It was now about noon, and darkness covered the whole earth until about three o'clock, while the sun stopped shining" (Luke 23:44-45). Did this literally happen? Or was Luke using this detail to point to something deeper? The Gospel writers were not simply reporters. They tried to help their hearers to feel, to experience, and to know the truth of what happened in Jesus's life and ministry.

What happened in Jerusalem and the surrounding area from noon to 3 on the day Jesus was crucified? What does Luke mean by telling us there were three hours of darkness? Some think it was an eclipse, except eclipses last, perhaps, seven minutes. Some say God miraculously stopped the earth from spinning and locked the moon into place. But the earth spins at one thousand miles per hour at its equator and stopping the earth would have had catastrophic consequences. I suspect it was dark clouds that rolled in—so that the atmospheric conditions reflected what was happening at Calvary that day. I also wonder if the real point Mark was trying to make, with Luke and Matthew drawing upon his account, was not intending to describe an astronomical or meteorological event but was instead trying to describe a spiritual and moral darkness that descended on the earth on the day when humans tortured the incarnate Son of God to death. It is likely that we may miss the significance of the darkness if we're merely worried about, as some have been, explaining the physics of how God caused the sun to stop shining. The point the Gospel writers were making is that it was a dark day for all creation when Jesus suffered and died. The day Jesus was crucified was a dark day for humankind and our world. The hour he died was a dark hour.

On February 24, 2022, Russia attacked Ukraine. The attack on Mariupol was especially horrific. The Russian army besieged the city and utterly destroyed it. AP reporters described the casualties of this city, so devastated by Russian forces, and the children who died there. A mother who had just lost a toddler held him and cried out, "Why? Why? Why?" The journalists described her at the hospital, holding him, kissing him, "inhaling his scent one last time." They wrote, "That was the day the darkness settled in for good."[4] The reporters spoke of darkness in a way similar to what Luke may have done as he was describing cosmic grief over Christ's crucifixion. It seemed that "darkness settled in for good" on that day. The one who came to lift up the lowly, who offered mercy and grace to the sinner, healing and life for the broken, hung dying on the cross. The source of light would shine no more.

During Good Friday worship services at Church of the Resurrection, we extinguish the Christ candle we lit on Christmas Eve. We do this to convey the darkness that covered the land as the Son of God hung dying on the cross.

The Curtain in the Temple Torn in Two

Luke also notes that the curtain in the Temple was torn apart from top to bottom. This curtain separated the throne room of God, the Holy of Holies, from the rest of the Temple. It was a thick tapestry, said to be as thick as a person's hand, sixty feet tall and thirty feet wide. It must have been beautiful. This tapestry separated the "throne room" of God from the common people. The rending of the curtain may have signified that Christ's death tore down the wall that separated humanity from God. Once more we might ask, Did this literally happen, or is Luke trying to tell us something about Jesus's death, or is there something more going on here?

Interpreters are divided on the meaning of the curtain tearing, but here are several thoughts about its significance.

Some see it as a foreshadowing of what is to come in Jerusalem given that the religious leaders rejected Jesus's call to love their enemies and to turn the other cheek. Since they did not pursue this path, a violent uprising will occur. Jesus knows this, and he knows that the Temple will be destroyed in Rome's attempt to crush this rebellion. It is for this reason Jesus wept as he entered Jerusalem.

Others see the tearing of this curtain as a way of expressing that, in Jesus's death, the curtain that separated humanity from God, which literally separated the Holy of Holies and the people in the Temple, has been destroyed due to the atoning death of Jesus.

Still others see this rending of the Temple's curtain as a sign of God's anger over what was done to Jesus and a way of suggesting that God has left his Temple and his people in response to the tragic death of Jesus. There are other interpretations, and I encourage you to explore them as you reflect on this story. As you reflect upon this, what do you think the significance of this detail is?

Father, Into Your Hands, I Entrust My Life

That takes us to the final words of Jesus from the cross in Luke's Gospel, a second prayer, this one drawn from Psalm 31. He prays, "Father, *into your hands I entrust my life*" (Luke 23:46). Other translations read, "into your hands I commit my spirit" (NIV).

In his darkest moment, in the midst of the pain, uncertain precisely what will happen next, as the crowd insults him, as his enemies gloat over him, as his body fails him, Jesus prays, "Father, into your hands I commit my spirit."

As we've learned, Luke emphasizes Jesus's practices of prayer. It is instructive that two of Jesus's three statements from the cross in Luke's Gospel are prayers. He prays first for his enemies: "Father, forgive them, for they don't know what they're doing" (23:34). His final words on the cross, according to Luke, are also a prayer, but this time, Jesus prays using words from the Psalms, specifically Psalm 31:5: "Into your hands I commit my spirit" (NIV).

> As we pray the Psalms or other scriptures, we join in a spiritual practice so important to Jesus that he practiced it even while dying on the cross.

In Matthew and Mark, we hear Jesus pray from the cross, "My God, my God, why have you forsaken me?" This is also a verse from the Psalms—Psalm 22:1. What we learn from both of these final words from Jesus is that he prayed the Psalms. This is a powerful practice. You've likely done this with Psalm 23, "The Lord is my shepherd..." If you haven't tried this with other psalms, I encourage you to do so. Read a psalm or portion of a psalm each day, and when you come to a verse or line that speaks to you, offer it as a prayer to God. I often start my times of prayer with Psalm 100. When confessing to God, I might use a part of Psalm 51. There are so many other deeply meaningful verses in the Psalms that we might so easily pray. My pocket Testament has underlines and brackets around hundreds of these lines or verses in the Psalms. And as we pray the Psalms or other scriptures, we join in a spiritual practice so important to Jesus that he practiced it even while dying on the cross.

William Barclay said that these words of Psalm 31:5, which Jesus now prayed, were a bedtime prayer every Jewish mother taught her children to pray. We might compare it to a prayer many Christian mothers used to teach their children to pray, "Now I lay me down to sleep…" What a deeply moving picture this is as we imagine Mary, Jesus's mother, standing at his feet (as John's Gospel tells us that she was), and Mary hears her son's final prayer, the prayer that she had taught him as a child. "Jesus called out with a loud voice, 'Father, into your hands I commit my spirit.' When he had said this, he breathed his last" (Luke 23:46 NIV).

What if you took these words of Jesus, and of King David, and regularly made them your prayer? When you are afraid: "Father, into your hands I commit my spirit." When you are in danger: "Father, into your hands I commit my spirit." When you are sick or preparing for surgery: "Father, into your hands I commit my spirit." When you feel hopeless: "Father, into your hands I commit my spirit." Or what if, every night before you went to bed, you joined Jesus in praying, "Father, into your hands I commit my spirit"?

Jesus's Death

There has been some debate among scholars regarding Luke's view of the meaning of Jesus's death. Some suggest that Luke does not see Jesus's death as atoning for sin—the handful of verses that might point to Jesus's death for our sin, it is noted, do not appear in some of the earliest Greek manuscripts of Luke. Jesus, according to some of these scholars, dies in faithfulness to God, or as a demonstration of his obedience to God, or to identify with our humanity—that is, our human experience of injustice, suffering, and death. There are other ways they explain the significance of Jesus's death in Luke. And it is in his resurrection that he defeats death and triumphs over evil, hate, sin, and suffering. I'm not doing justice to the argument, but I want you to know that this has been the source of some debate among scholars.

Whether you agree with these scholars concerning Luke's view of atonement or not, throughout Luke we do see the emphasis is on Jesus's ministry, compassion, and mercy as bringing salvation or deliverance and forgiveness, and he brings these quite apart from his death. Even on the cross, he has announced salvation to the thief at his side *before he dies*. His death does, however, move us to repentance.

Having said that, Luke may be hinting at atonement in various ways in his Gospel. When Jesus says that he would be numbered among the outlaws, he is quoting Isaiah 53, a chapter that may have initially referred to Israel's suffering at the hands of her enemies, but which Christians clearly saw as pointing to Jesus's suffering and death for us. We may see a hint of atonement when Pilate releases Barabbas while sending Jesus to be put to death. Jesus dies and a criminal goes free. This is, perhaps, a foreshadowing of the idea of Christ dying, not just for Barabbas, but for humanity. We may see atonement as Jesus hangs on the cross praying, "Father, forgive them, for they don't know what they are doing" (a passage that is also absent from some ancient manuscripts). Here Jesus acts as priest, praying for mercy and atonement for those who murdered him. This might be a nuanced way for Luke to portray Jesus as both priest and atoning sacrifice.

Regardless of what Luke was seeking to convey about Jesus's death, he clearly sees this as the climax of the story he has been telling. Here, too, Jesus is lifting up the lowly. In Jesus's death, we see his obedience to God ("not my will but thy will be done"), his innocent suffering, and, once again, his ministry with and for the outsiders, outcasts, and outlaws. We see his mercy and grace as he prays for his Father to forgive even those who tortured him.

We see him reaching out to "seek and save the lost," even from the cross. We see him as a King suffering for his people—a picture of selfless love. And we see Jesus absorbing evil, hate, sin, and death. As we will see in the postscript, Jesus ultimately triumphs over these things, and in the process brings salvation to the world.

POSTSCRIPT

THE CRUCIFIED AND RESURRECTED LIFE

*Very early in the morning on the first day of the week, the women went to the tomb, bringing the fragrant spices they had prepared. They found the stone rolled away from the tomb, but when they went in, they didn't find the body of the Lord Jesus. They didn't know what to make of this. Suddenly, two men were standing beside them in gleaming bright clothing. The women were frightened and bowed their faces toward the ground, but the men said to them, "Why do you look for the living among the dead? He isn't here, but has been raised. Remember what he told you while he was still in Galilee, that the Human One must be handed over to sinners, **be crucified, and on the third day rise again.**" Then they remembered his words. When they returned from the tomb, they reported all these things to the eleven and all the others. It was Mary Magdalene, Joanna, Mary the mother of James, and the other women with them who told these things to the apostles. Their words struck the apostles as nonsense, and they didn't believe the women.*

(Luke 24:1-11, emphasis added)

I remember, as I began reading the Gospels as a fourteen-year-old atheist, that their stories about Jesus led me to admire him, then to love him, then to wish to follow him. But there was one story that I struggled to believe. It was the story of the Resurrection. I read Matthew and came to the Resurrection and thought, "This is clearly mythical. I can't make myself believe that Jesus died, was buried, and walked out of the tomb thirty-six hours later.[1] Then I read Mark with its shorter original ending where the women found an empty tomb and heard from a "young man dressed in white" that Jesus had been raised. I remember thinking, "I wish it happened that way, but I just can't buy the Resurrection story." And then I read Luke's Gospel. The story was just as unbelievable, but for the first time it made sense. It seemed logically essential to Jesus's story. In this postscript we explore Luke's unique account of the Easter story, and when I conclude this chapter I'll tell you why the Resurrection suddenly made sense to me.

Jesus's Burial

Following Jesus's death, all four Gospels tell us that a man named Joseph of Arimathea approached Pontius Pilate and requested the right to remove Jesus's body from the cross and to give him a proper burial. The fact that all four Gospels tell this story, and in mostly the same details, points to the importance of this scene for early Christians and how widely known this story was in first-century Christianity. The various Gospels tell us different details to serve each of the author's purposes.

Matthew calls Joseph a "rich man" who had become a disciple of Jesus and tells us that he buries Jesus in his own tomb (Matthew 27:57-60). But Matthew does not tell us Joseph was a member of the Jewish council. Mark tells us that "Joseph was a prominent council member who also eagerly anticipated the coming of God's kingdom" (Mark 15:43). He doesn't mention that the tomb was Joseph's. Luke doesn't tell us he was rich but does include that he was a member of the council, and Luke adds, "He was a good and righteous man. He hadn't agreed with the plan and actions of the council" (Luke 23:50-51). John joins Matthew in mentioning that "Joseph was a disciple of Jesus," and he adds, "but a secret one because he feared the Jewish authorities." He continues, "Nicodemus, the one who at first had come to Jesus at night, was there too. He brought a mixture of myrrh and aloe, nearly seventy-five pounds in all." John tells us the setting of Jesus's burial, "There was a garden in the place where Jesus was crucified, and in the garden was a new tomb in which no one had ever been laid" (John 19:38-42).[2]

Put them all together and, in Joseph, we have a picture of a righteous man who found his courage, as Jesus was crucified, to no longer keep his sympathy with and faith in Jesus hidden. Here we find one of the places where a Jewish religious leader who is a wealthy man gets it right in Luke, and in so doing he risks his status, breaking rank with the rest of the Jewish ruling council. He becomes an outsider as a result of his care for Jesus. Joseph becomes a model of discipleship here, at Jesus's death, when he finally, publicly, and likely at no small cost, identifies himself as a follower of Jesus. I wonder, are you willing to risk the approval of family, coworkers, and friends by identifying as a follower of Jesus?

The Women at the Tomb

The male disciples had fled at Jesus's arrest in Gethsemane. But the women who had followed Jesus in and from Galilee also followed Jesus to the cross (Luke 23:27-31). They watched Jesus's crucifixion "from a distance" (Luke 23:49). The women followed Joseph to the tomb. "They saw the tomb and how Jesus' body was laid in it, then they went away and prepared fragrant spices and perfumed oils" (Luke 23:55-56). The Sabbath started at sunset on that Friday night, so the women went to the place where they were staying, planning to return after the Sabbath was over, early on the first day of the week (Sunday).

Luke begins his telling of the Easter story with these women:

Very early in the morning on the first day of the week, the women went to the tomb, bringing the fragrant spices they had prepared. They found the stone rolled away from the tomb, but when they went in, they didn't find the body of the Lord Jesus. They didn't know what to make of this. (Luke 24:1-4a)

Once again, we find women playing a pivotal role in the Gospel of Luke. They had courage to follow Jesus all the way to the cross (Peter had promised this, but his courage had failed). They alone saw where his body was laid. They were the first to return to the tomb with plans to have the stone rolled away to finish the burial preparations. And, as they came to the tomb on that first Easter morning, they became the first to learn that Jesus had been raised.

They rushed back to the disciples who were in hiding. And now they became the first to proclaim the good news of the Resurrection. Women were first entrusted with this message. And not just any women; it was women out of whom Jesus had cast out demons and otherwise healed. While women are often left unnamed in the Bible, Luke gives us these women's names: "It was Mary Magdalene, Joanna, Mary the mother of James, and the other women with them who told these things to the apostles" (Luke 24:10). But, Luke notes, "their words struck the apostles as nonsense, and they didn't believe the women" (24:11). I'm reminded that first-century Jews did not consider women reliable witnesses. Yet God lifted up the lowly, honoring them by allowing them to be the first to know that Christ was raised and the first to proclaim that "Christ is risen!" As I noted earlier in the book, Luke's special eyewitness source for some of his material may well have been the recollections of these women.

Remember that in Luke, it was a woman, Elizabeth, who first called Jesus Lord. It is women who are most prominent in the birth narratives, whose voices and songs we hear. We hear of the frequent healing of women. Jesus eats in the home of two women. Women fund his ministry. Women follow Jesus to the cross. And women are the first to bear witness to the Resurrection.

Even in his resurrection, Jesus lifts up the voices and importance of women.

The Crucifixion
and the Crucified Life

One year during Holy Week, I received an email from one of our church members whose dad had died unexpectedly a few months earlier. He wrote,

> Easter means more this year than it ever has. I think of
> my dad's life's arc and how after meeting my mother, he
> truly began his faith journey. From that point on, it was
> faith that defined all other points of meaning in his life...
> I miss him terribly, but I absolutely know I will see him
> again, hear his laugh and his voice. It's not just a hope, it's
> an almost certainty and a trust.

The resurrection of Jesus makes clear one essential truth about life as seen through the Christian faith: life includes crucifixion moments, moments of adversity, suffering, and death, *but none of these has the final word in our lives*. Resurrection is the final word in the Gospel and in life. In literature, the term *denouement* means the final conclusion that resolves the conflicts in the story and helps everything else make sense. The resurrection is the denouement of the Gospel. Christ's resurrection, Easter, is God's way of saying crucifixion, suffering, tragedy, and pain don't have the final word. As Christians we live the crucified *and resurrected* life.

I've often been asked, "In the light of the terrible suffering and tragedies that happen in the world, how can we possibly believe in God?" I understand the question and the feeling. It is likely that you have wondered the same when struggling with illness or experiencing cruelty or injustice or unfair suffering. We've all known crucifixion moments. We've all felt like crying out, "My God, my God, why have your forsaken me?"

Our disappointment with God often comes from our expectations of how God works in the world. We often believe that God should and would stop powerful people from waging war against their neighbors. We assume that if God is good, he would prevent school shootings or acts of terrorism, prevent cancer, and eradicate COVID-19 and every other kind of sickness. If God was good, and real, God would keep our hearts from being broken and we'd never be disappointed. He'd stop the storms and give us blue skies and seventy-five-degree temperatures every day.

But the crucifixion of Jesus makes clear that this is not how the world works, not even when God himself walked on this earth in Jesus. Suffering is a part of life. Crucifixion is where God, in the person of Jesus, joins us in our suffering. We all will live, at points, a crucified life. We'll all know moments of unjust suffering and heartache and pain. But in Easter Christ triumphs over the crucified life and promises that we, too, will triumph. That trust in Easter, not merely believing in it, but counting on it, changes our perspective on life, suffering, adversity, and death.

The Walk to Emmaus: Breaking Bread with the Stranger

As Luke continues the story of Easter, he once more offers us a story not found in any other Gospel (though the latter addition to Mark includes a hint of it—see Mark 16:12-13). That first Easter, though knowing the tomb had been opened and Jesus's body was no longer there, the male disciples had not believed the report of the women that Jesus had been raised. The women themselves had not yet seen Jesus but were trusting the words of two men "standing beside them in gleaming bright clothing" (Luke 24:4). In the disciples' disbelief, things had gone from bad to worse. Jesus had been crucified and buried, and someone had broken in the tomb and taken his body.

This was the situation when two of the men, a previously unnamed disciple named Cleopas and another who remains unnamed, decided to go back to their home in a nearby town called Emmaus, about a two-hour walk away. As they walked home in their grief, a stranger approached and joined them on their journey. The man asked, "'What are you talking about as you walk along?' They stopped, their faces downcast" (Luke 24:17). As they continued to walk, they told this stranger all that had happened to Jesus, and how they had "hoped he was the one who would redeem Israel" (24:21). The stranger replied:

> *"You foolish people! Your dull minds keep you from believing all that the prophets talked about. Wasn't it necessary for the Christ to suffer these things and then enter into his glory?" Then he interpreted for them the things written about himself in all the scriptures, starting with Moses and going through all the Prophets.*
>
> *(Luke 24:25-27)*

As they arrived at Emmaus, their home, "he acted as if he was going on ahead." I love this, he was testing these two disciples. "But they urged him, saying, 'Stay with us. It's nearly evening, and the day is almost over.' So he went in to stay with them" (Luke 24:28-29). This is such a great story! They invite him in, sit down to eat with him, and invite him to offer the blessing over the meal. "He took the bread, blessed and broke it, and gave it to them. Their eyes were opened and they recognized him, but he disappeared from their sight" (24:30-31). The stranger, they now see, was Jesus!

I am reminded of Matthew 25 when Jesus spoke of the Last Judgment and described the criteria for entering into God's eternal kingdom: "I was hungry and you gave me food to eat....I was a stranger and you welcomed me" (25:35). It is impossible to miss the allusion to Holy Communion in these verses from Luke. These disciples had eaten with Jesus many times. But it was as they broke bread with him now that their eyes were opened. Or, as Luke notes in 24:35, "Jesus was made known to them as he broke the bread." Luke was pointing to the ongoing revelation of Jesus to believers as they share in Holy Communion. When we share in the Eucharist we remember and become a part of all the meals that Jesus shared—we are part of the multitude Jesus fed with the fish and the loaves. We remember Jesus's words at one such miracle when Jesus said, "I am the bread of life. Whoever comes to me will never go hungry" (John 6:35). We are with Jesus at the Last Supper, remembering that this bread and wine were given for us, and his words that the truly great will be servants. And we join Cleopas and the unnamed disciple in having our eyes opened and seeing Jesus in the breaking of the bread.

The Passover meal functions similarly for Jewish people. The meal transports Jewish families back to Egypt. They remember that they once were slaves. They see God's deliverance and become a part of God's liberated people.

These disciples returned with haste to Jerusalem to tell the others that what the women had said was true, that Jesus was indeed raised from the dead.

Don't miss, in this story, that the resurrected Christ came as a stranger. How sad it would have been if those two disciples had said, as he began to walk along with them, "Friend, we're having a private conversation. We're grieving, can you leave us alone?" Or if, when they had arrived in Emmaus they had simply said their goodbyes without insisting that Jesus stay with them for the night and join them at the supper table. I wonder how often we miss encounters with Jesus because we're not paying attention, or we're too busy or preoccupied? I don't mean that we literally miss the resurrected Jesus coming to us, though that is possible; but by not paying attention or welcoming strangers, we miss moments where we might have an experience with him, or hear him speak to us, through the very human strangers we welcome.

Luke's Easter and Christian Worship

Fred Craddock, in his commentary on Luke, named something other scholars have suggested as well, something even the casual reader senses when reading the Emmaus story: Luke's account of Easter hints at the structure and form of Christian worship, and this might be Luke's intention.

The Easter story begins with angels, and then the women, proclaiming that "Christ is risen"—an *affirmation of faith*. It progresses to two disciples hearing the stranger on the road to Emmaus where Jesus "interpreted for them the things written about himself in all the scriptures, starting with Moses and going through all the Prophets" (Luke 24:27). In Christian worship, this is the *sermon or homily*. Upon arriving in Emmaus, "he took the bread, blessed and broke it, and gave it to them. Their eyes were opened and they recognized him" (24:30-31)—*the Eucharist* in worship.

Listen to what happens next in Luke's account that first Easter: "While they were saying these things, Jesus himself stood among them and said, 'Peace be with you!'" (Luke 24:36). In worship, Christ is in our midst (this is explicit in Matthew 18:20 where Jesus said, "Where two or three are gathered in my name, I'm there with them"). In many congregations, members greet one another saying, "The peace of Christ be yours." This is called the "*passing of the peace*." Jesus then commissions his disciples noting, "You are witnesses of these things" (Luke 24:48). He tells them that the story must be told and repentance preached. Every weekend in worship the service ends with the "*sending forth*" as the church is sent to be "witnesses of these things."

On that first Easter, Jesus sends out a group of largely uneducated, common, *'Am ha-Arez* to proclaim the good news and to change the world. And he still does this every time we gather for worship. Christians began worshipping on Sundays because it was on that day that Jesus rose from the dead, and our worship is, in some way, a remembering and reenactment of what happened on that first Easter morning.

Notice how Luke's Gospel ends, with Jesus's ascension:

> He led them out as far as Bethany, where he lifted his hands and blessed them. As he blessed them, he left them and was taken up to heaven. They worshipped him and returned to Jerusalem overwhelmed with joy. And they were continuously in the temple praising God.
>
> *(Luke 24:51-53)*

Jesus ascended to heaven, but before he did he commissioned and blessed the disciples. They worshipped him and returned to their home "overwhelmed with joy." And they continuously praised God. We're meant to encounter Jesus every week in worship, affirming our faith in him who conquered death; we're meant to study the scriptures as we reflect upon his life; we're meant to share together in the Eucharist, meeting him in the breaking of the bread; we're meant to experience his presence and his peace and to hear his call upon us to be his witnesses. Having been blessed by him, we return to our homes with joy.

The resurrection of Christ changed everything for these disciples. Seeing Jesus raised from the dead lifted them up when they were low, grief-stricken, and fearful. The Resurrection brought them joy instead of sorrow. It gave them hope in place of despair. It gave them peace and courage instead of fear.

This is the crucified and resurrected life.

The Meaning of the Cross and Resurrection

The New Testament has different ways of attempting to explain the meaning of Jesus's death. Early Christians used different metaphors to describe it. Christ gave himself as a ransom to buy our freedom; he offered himself as an atoning sacrifice procuring our forgiveness; he bore the punishment we deserve for sins he didn't commit. He purchases us or redeems us. He takes our place in receiving the just penalty for sin. The cross was a picture of God's love and a picture of the selfless love God calls us to.

And these are just a few of the ways the New Testament speaks of the meaning of Christ's death. But there's another: Jesus taking on the powers of darkness, being apparently defeated by them on the cross, and in his resurrection, ultimately defeating them.

In Eugene Peterson's translation of Colossians 2:15 he writes, "[Jesus] stripped all the spiritual tyrants in the universe of their sham authority at the Cross and marched them naked through the streets" (MSG). Swedish theologian Gustaf Aulen, back in 1930, gave a name to this way of thinking about Christ's death and resurrection. He called it "Christ the Victor."[3] He noted that this idea was perhaps the leading view of the significance of Jesus's death and resurrection through much of church history. On the cross, Christ had battled with the forces of darkness and appeared to have been defeated by them. But in his resurrection, he demonstrated his victory over hate, evil, sin, and death.

This is what's behind something Frederick Buechner once said, which has come to define the power of Easter for me, something I share with the Church of the Resurrection each year at Easter: "Resurrection means the worst thing is never the last thing." As I was preparing the final revisions to this book, Frederick Buechner, pastor, theologian, and writer, died at the age of ninety-six. It struck me as I heard this news that on that day, for Buechner, it was so very true that the worst thing was not the last thing. Death did not have the final word for Buechner, just as it will not for you. In Jesus's death and resurrection, light conquers darkness, love vanquishes hate, and life defeats death. The death and resurrection of Jesus shows us that these powers of darkness, evil, sin, sickness, tragedy, and death will ultimately be defeated.

This is God's final act of lifting up the lowly. Jesus identified with our pain and suffering. He became an outsider, an outcast, and an outlaw for us. But in his resurrection, he lifts us out of the depths and gives us love, joy, and peace.

This is what I came to understand that night when I was fourteen years old as I finished reading the Gospel of Luke. I had come to love Jesus because of his love for the nobodies and how he made friends in "low places." But that night, reading Luke 24, the Resurrection finally made sense. In fact, it was a logical necessity. If Jesus had come from God, was in fact God enfleshed, his story could not end with his death. To end at the tomb would have meant that cruelty, inhumanity, evil, tragedy, sin, darkness, and death do in fact have the final word. It would mean that the powers of darkness had defeated the Light of the World. But in the Resurrection, God powerfully demonstrated that love, light, and life have definitively defeated tragedy, evil, and death.

I closed my Bible, got down on my knees next to my bed, and I prayed, "Jesus, I want to follow you. I want to be your disciple. I know I'm just a kid, just fourteen, but if you can use me, please do. I offer my life to you." I've been saying some version of that prayer every day since.

Luke's portrayal of Jesus changed my life. Through his words I came to know and love Jesus, and committed my life to following him. My hope in writing this book was that each reader who has felt like an outsider, outcast, or outlaw might meet Jesus in Luke's Gospel. I hope that you would choose to follow him, knowing he came for people just like you. And for those of you who are already Christ-followers, I hope that you might find, like Theophilus to whom the gospel was written, that in studying Luke, you have "confidence in the soundness of the instruction you have received" (Luke 1:4).

I'd like to invite you to make this your prayer:

Jesus, thank you for lifting up the lowly, and for loving the outsiders, the outcasts, and the outlaws. I want to follow you, to be your disciple. If you can use me, please do. I offer my life to you. Amen.

ACKNOWLEDGMENTS

I've dedicated this book to the church that welcomed me as a fourteen-year-old outsider and helped me to know Christ. In particular I want to acknowledge Rev. Phil Hollis and Rev. Gary Patterson, who were pastor and youth pastor at the time. Though they are both with Christ, I continue to be grateful for the role they played in helping me know Christ and to grow in my faith.

I'm profoundly grateful for the people of The United Methodist Church of the Resurrection who allow me to write. This book is the culmination of several sermon series on Luke that I've preached over the years. I'm so proud of the people of this congregation and the ways they seek to embody the Gospel of Luke.

This book would not have been possible were it not for the amazing team at Abingdon Press. Thank you to Susan Salley, the Associate Publisher at Abingdon, who leads the team I work with. Susan, you are a great collaborator and friend! I'm grateful for Brian Sigmon who serves as the editor for my books. Brian you are a gift from God. Thank you for all you do to make my books better! And thanks for your patience when I miss deadlines! Thank you to Tim Cobb who tirelessly oversees the production process, including the maps, images, and illustrations that enrich the book. Thanks also to the marketing team who go above and beyond to help this book and others reach an audience of new and longtime readers. And thank you to Tracey Craddock, Andrew Weitze, and others at Abingdon who worked on this book and the accompanying video and study materials.

LUKE

I want to thank my wife and best friend, LaVon Bandy Hamilton. After 40 years of marriage, I truly love you more than ever. Thank you for your patience and support. The hours spent writing this book were taken directly from time we would have had together. Your investment in each of my books is significant. Thank you.

NOTES

<hr>

Introduction

1   Paul is the stated author of Colossians (Colossians 1:1 and 4:18). Many mainline scholars believe it was written after the time of Paul by one of his followers who sought to apply Paul's words and message to a generation sometime after Paul's death. Either way, Colossians and 2 Timothy, of which the same is thought, record the place Luke played in the life of Paul and the early church.

1. Lifting Up the Lowly

1   Steve Cavendish, "The Fight to Be a Middle-Aged Female News Anchor," *New York Times*, March 11, 2019, Opinion, https://www.nytimes .com/2019/03/11/opinion/meredith-kalodimos-age-discrimination.html.

2   The Greek word *tekton* was used by the Gospel writers to describe Joseph. It could be translated as carpenter, but most homes were built with stone and another Greek term was typically used for stonemason. A *tekton* would have fixed things, made farm implements, doors, and furniture.

3   There's far more I've written about this in various books including *Prepare the Way for the Lord*. Every one of us needs an Elizabeth, an older and wiser mentor. And all of us need a Mary, a younger person we seek to bless, encourage, and mentor. Who is your Mary? Who is your Elizabeth?

4   *Jewish Encyclopedia,* s.v. "'AM HA-AREZ, by Kaufmann Kohler," accessed August 22, 2022, https://www.jewishencyclopedia.com /articles/1356-am-ha-arez.

5   "'AM HA-AREZ."

2. Simon, Do You See This Woman?

1   "Employment and Earnings by Occupation," The Women's Bureau, an agency in the US Department of Labor, https://www.dol.gov /agencies/wb/data/occupations. Pew suggests eighty-four cents per dollar men earned: "Gender Pay Gap in U.S. Held Steady in 2020," by Amanda Barroso and Anna Brown, https://www.pewresearch.org /fact-tank/2021/05/25/gender-pay-gap-facts/.

2   "Victims of Sexual Violence: Statistics," RAINN (Rape, Abuse & Incest National Network), accessed August 24, 2022, https://www.rainn .org/statistics/victims-sexual-violence.

3   "A New Survey Finds 81 Percent of Women Have Experienced Sexual Harassment," narrated by Rhitu Chatterjee, NPR, *The Two-Way*, February 21, 2018, https://www.npr.org/sections /thetwo-way/2018/02/21/587671849/a-new-survey-finds-eighty -percent-of-women-have-experienced-sexual-harassment.

4   Sandra Percy, quoted in Greg W. Forbes and Scott D. Harrower, *Raised from Obscurity: A Narratival and Theological Study of the Characterization of Women in Luke-Acts* (Eugene, OR: Pickwick Publications, 2015), 21, Kindle.

5   Philo, *On the Embassy to Gaius*, paragraph 319 found here: http:// www.earlychristianwritings.com/yonge/book40.html.

6   Josephus, *Antiquities*, 4:219.

7   Rabbi Eliezar in M. Sotah 3:4. This and some of the other references from Forbes et al.

8   M. 'Abot 1:4-5 quoted in *The New Interpreter's Bible Commentary*, ed. Leander Keck, (Nashville: Abingdon Press, vol. 9, 2015), 231. See footnote there.

9   David Garland, *Luke: Zondervan Exegetical Commentary on the New Testament* (Grand Rapids, MI: Zondervan, 2011), 453.

10 The church statistic comes from the 2020 Church and Tax Law survey. The 17.5 percent includes volunteers, staff, and pastors who had experienced harassment from church members, staff, and pastors.

3. Parables from the Underside

1   "Signs of Decline and Hope Among Key Metrics of Faith," in Barna: State of the Church 2020, March 4, 2020, https://www.barna.com /research/changing-state-of-the-church/.

2   There are some who also see this name and story as tied to the story of
    Jesus's friend, Lazarus, who was raised from the dead in John's Gospel.
    Were these two stories somehow remembered in different ways?
    Similarly, the story of Mary and Martha is attached to Lazarus in
    John but Lazarus is not mentioned in Luke's story of the sisters.

3   "The Duty of Newspapers Is to Comfort the Afflicted and to Afflict
    the Comfortable," October 4, 1902, *The Province*, Mr. Dooley on
    Newspaper Publicity by F. P. Dunne, quote p. 6, col. 1, Vancouver,
    British Columbia, Canada (Newspapers.com), *Quote Investigator*,
    https://quoteinvestigator.com/2019/02/01/comfort/.

4. On the Journey to Jerusalem

1   Quoted by Kauffman Kohler in " 'AM HA-AREZ."

2   Garland, *Luke*, 729.

3   Joseph A. Fitzmyer, SJ, *The Gospel According to Luke X–XXIV*, Yale
    Anchor Bible Commentary (New York: Doubleday, 1985), 2:817.

5. The Final Week

1   "Ancient Jewish History: The Beit Din," https://www.jewishvirtuallibrary
    .org/the-beit-din.

2   Martin Luther King Jr., "Where Do We Go from Here?" speech to the
    Southern Christian Leadership Conference, Atlanta, Georgia, August 16,
    1967, https://www.youtube.com/watch?v=yeVITdHsY6I.

6. Crucified with the Outlaws

1   Saugato Biswas, Trupti Surana, Abhishek De, and Falguni Nag, "A
    Curious Case of Sweating Blood," *Indian Journal of Dermatology*
    (58, no. 6 (Nov.–Dec. 2013); 478–480.

2   Matthew, Mark, and Luke combine to say that Jesus hung on the cross
    from 9 to 3. John says that he was crucified about noon, not 9 a.m.

3   "Tears, Forgiveness, as Rochester Man Pleads Guilty to Killing
    Community Activist's Father in DWI Crash," WHEC, Rochester, NY,
    April 4, 2022, updated July 27, 2022, https://www.whec.com/archive
    /tears-forgiveness-as-rochester-man-pleads-guilty-to-killing-community
    -activists-father-in-dwi-crash/.

4   Mstyslav Chernov, Evgeniy Maloletka, and Lori Hinnant, " 'Why? Why?
    Why?' Ukraine's Mariupol Descends into Despair," *AP News*, March
    16, 2022, https://apnews.com/article/russia-ukraine-war-mariupol
    -descends-into-despair-708cb8f4a171ce1b0b8d090e38e3.

Notes

Postscript

1   Though only thirty-six hours, it was three days by Jewish reckoning as Jesus died on Friday (day one) remained in the tomb on Saturday (day two) and was raised on Sunday (day three).

2   For John, the garden is a critically important key to understanding the meaning of Jesus's death and resurrection. John begins with a nod to Genesis 1, "In the beginning." And Genesis begins in a garden where ultimately, due to humans turning away from God, they are banished from paradise and death is a curse that results. In John's account, Jesus is crucified in a garden, buried in a garden, raised in a garden, and he appears as a gardener to Mary. He is reversing the events that happened in the first garden. See my book *John: Gospel of Light and Life* for more information.

3   Gustaf Aulen, *Christus Victor: An Historical Study of the Three Main Types of the Idea of Atonement* (Eugene, OR: Wipf and Stock, 2003).

ABOUT THE COVER ARTIST

IVAN FILICHEV
(1937-2021)

Filichev was born in Bezhitsa, Russia, in 1937, and he grew up during Joseph Stalin's regime. Filichev's early art was influenced by a love of the paintings of the Itinerants, a nineteenth-century Russian school of realist painters. His formal art training was at the Yelets Fine Art College and Kharkov Fine Art-Industrial Institute. Most of Filichev's work with religious themes were painted after 1988 during Russia's new era of religious tolerance. Most of his religious art relies upon abstract figures in high contrast colors with minimal use of whitewash. Among those credited with influencing his religious art are Theophanes the Greek, El Greco, and Paul Cezanne. Filichev is an honored Artist of Russia with works in museums in Russia, Ukraine, Great Britain, and private collections around the world.

**To see more art by Ivan Filichev,
visit ivan-filichev.pixels.com.**

Watch videos based on *Luke: Jesus and the Outsiders, Outcasts, and Outlaws* with Adam Hamilton through Amplify Media.

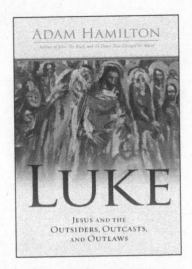

Amplify Media is a multimedia platform that delivers high quality, searchable content with an emphasis on Wesleyan perspectives for churchwide, group, or individual use on any device at any time. In a world of sometimes overwhelming choices, Amplify gives church leaders and congregants media capabilities that are contemporary, relevant, effective, and, most importantly, affordable and sustainable.

With **Amplify Media** church leaders can:

- Provide a reliable source of Christian content through a Wesleyan lens for teaching, training, and inspiration in a customizable library
- Deliver their own preaching and worship content in a way the congregation knows and appreciates
- Build the church's capacity to innovate with engaging content and accessible technology
- Equip the congregation to better understand the Bible and its application
- Deepen discipleship beyond the church walls

Ask your group leader or pastor about Amplify Media and sign up today at www.AmplifyMedia.com.